Tradition and
Transformation
in Religious Education

Tradition and Transformation in Religious Education

edited by
PADRAIC O'HARE

ERRATUM. The title on the book
cover is inaccurately printed. The
correct title appears on this page.

Religious Education Press
Birmingham, Alabama

Library of Congress Cataloging in Publication Data

Main entry under title:

Tradition and transformation in religious education.

  Includes bibliographical references and index.
  1. Religious education—Congresses. I. O'Hare,
Padraic.
BL42.T72   207   78-27506
ISBN 0-89135-016-0

10 9 8 7 6 5 4 3 2

Religious Education Press, Inc.
1531 Wellington Rd.
Birmingham, Alabama 35209

*Religious Education Press publishes books and educational materials exclusively
in religious education and in areas closely related to religious education. It is
committed to enhancing and professionalizing religious education through the
publication of significant scholarly and popular works.*

Contents

Introduction

Padraic O'Hare

The tension in religious education between handing on tradition and changing the world (or between tradition and transformation as Boys frames it in her essay), is clearly addressed by the first four essays in this volume. Each of these essays rejects the notion of a conflict between tradition and transformation, finding warrant for education which is both inductive and humanistic[1] in the radical message of the tradition itself. All but Maria Harris find justification for this assertion in biblical faith—or Bible as exemplar of the intrinsic transformative character of tradition. Harris's contribution is altogether the most secular, fully a statement of *religious* as distinct from *Christian* education. For her, "word, "sacrament," and "prophecy" are transposed from ecclesial usage to serve as explanations of "the questions the ordinary life we lead raises."[2] Viewed from this perspective, Mary Boys's thesis may be characterized as truly eclectic, transcending the limits of a statement on Christian education (however rich) by her concern for the interpretative function of religious education (". . . The critical distance the hearers put between themselves and the narrative so as to determine the implications."). Letty Russell's approach is fully and intentionally Christocentric (educational ministry viewed as the invitation, "for youth

1

and old alike to try out the life story of Jesus in their lives"). And in Ellis Nelson's view—although it is sophisticated—tradition and Bible tend to collapse into one another. It should also be noted of Nelson's essay however, that it is the most refreshingly candid about the unlikelihood of an early solution to the tension between tradition and transformation, and the most attentive to the discipline of matters of fact.

Each of the authors presents a relatively full general definition of religious education, and therefore elements in these theses should not be viewed in isolation. However, several notable points in each of the essays may be highlighted with benefit. Boys's essay represents a sophisticated utilization of the technology of biblical criticism and redaction to demonstrate that in the process of "reactualizing" tradition, of ". . . selecting, combining, and rejecting components of tradition. . . ," tradition becomes transformative. This occurs precisely as we " . . . (acknowledge) that tradition is to be acted upon." The mode of apprehending and interpreting the past exemplified in the Bible, especially the prophets and Jesus, is offered as a paradigm for the religious educator.

Boys's distinction between religious education as a means of "access" rather than an ". . . actual means of transformation . . ." is especially welcome. The wholesale repudiation in our times of narrowly cognitive views of religious education, however welcome, has nevertheless resulted in education which is at once manipulative and romantic.

The issue of means of access versus means of transformation is—educationally—reducible to the question of appeal to intrinsic motives for learning versus external reinforcement. And, as Bruner has noted: "External reinforcement may indeed get a particular act going and may even lead to its repetition, but it does not nourish, reliably, the long course of learning by which man slowly builds in his own way a serviceable model of what the world is and what it can be."[3] Boys's nonhubristic perspective is welcome and needed.

Maria Harris's essay is distinctive for its illuminating typology of dimensions in religious education, and the very evocative elaboration on this typology.

Asserting that the central realities of religious experience should influence our understanding of its purpose and not simply be reduced to content areas, Harris mines the categories "word," "sacrament," and "prophecy" as catalysts of the "three gracious acts" of the religious educator: teaching, hallowing, and parable. In her elaboration of what is implied for education in these acts, Harris enriches and expands in a most creative way the traditional concerns for cognition (naming and journeying), affection (ordering and sacramentalizing), and volition (questioning and foolishness). One feels these categories need more systematic examination and integration, but they stand as imaginative challenges for the religious educator.

Nelson's essay is notable for—among other things—the presentation of biblical theophany as a model for religious education and his practical recommendations for educational ministry, chiefly attention to adult religious education. The theophany is always to a *person*, in a *situation*, about *events*, and directing to *action*. Like Harris's typology, Nelson's examination of theophany functions as a prescriptive schema for religious education activity.

As noted above, Russell's essay is chiefly characterizeable, at least in comparison, by its unselfconscious christological focus. There is an element of *sola gratia* running through the essay. But this is counterbalanced by a conviction that dialogical modalities, diakoniac life style and educational environment, and a sincere attempt to overcome the alienating dichotomies of life will enable the Christian educator and those with whom she/he serves to respond faithfully. Russell's description of the several dimensions of faith is a welcome corrective to the univocal frame of mind which occasionally besets the religious educator.

Dwayne Huebner's concluding essay, the fruit of critical reflection on the other four essays, is a challenging hermeneutical analysis of the other papers complete with "suspicion" and "restoration" (Ricoeur). While Boys, Harris, Nelson, and Russell cannot be expected to assume Huebner's agenda, his critique is powerful as he points to these, among other unattended issues: the need for an ideology critique of the interests (social and personal, ecclesial and academic), of religious education theorists; the need to explore the linkage between language about education and the religious and the experience of education and the religious; and, the need to forge a *public language* for expressing the experience of education and the religious. For me the most powerful example of the hermeneutical hiatus to which Huebner points is his critique of the very structure of the symposium from which this volume emanates. This conference failed to engage academics and practitioners in a common quest for a common language which truly links expression and experience. Such an enterprise might overcome the alienation of adopting positivist language or the bankruptcy of adopting radically subjective language in expressing our common task.

This book is the fruit of a symposium involving four prominent religious education leaders and an education professor who critically reacted to these four. Specifically this volume is the result of the second annual symposium on Foundations of Religious Education sponsored by Boston College's Institute of Religious Education and Pastoral Ministry. Without prejudice to the ultimate importance of the practice of religious education, these symposia have addressed themselves to the theoretical roots of the religious education enterprise, trusting that the scholarly products of the symposia participants are the result of a ripened integration of experience and reflection and therefore not "mere" speculation.

Whereas, the first symposium, acknowledging the plurality among Catholic practitioners and theoreticians,[4] confined itself to exploring the perspectives on religious education of Catholic scholars, the present volume represents a Christian ecumenical enterprise. Four religious educators, two Protestant, two Catholic, were asked to develop papers and participate in a two-day conference in April, 1978 entitled "Christian Education: Handing on Tradditions and Changing the World." The fifth paper is the product of a major United States philosopher of education reflecting critically on the analysis proposed by the four religious educators.

The panelists who presented papers during the symposium are: Mary C. Boys, Assistant Professor of Theology and Religious Education at Boston College; Maria Harris, Associate Professor of Religious Education at Andover Newton Theology School; C. Ellis Nelson, President and Professor of Christian Education at Louisville Presbyterian Theological Seminary (and past chairman of the Department of Religious Education at Union Theological Seminary in New York City); and Letty Russell, As-

sociate Professor of Theology at Yale Divinity School. The
critical reactor was Dwayne Huebner, Professor of Education at Teachers College, Columbia University.

The purpose of the Boston College symposia is
genuinely ministerial in character. Its sponsors do not consider the ideas dealt with simply self-authenticating (even
while they would resist the tyrannization of scholarship by
expectations of immediate utility). Reflection on the tension or contradiction between religious education's transmissive and transformative purposes is at least an important question in the practical order. "Traditionalist" (in the
sense in which Boys employs the term) religious education
does not save tradition or incline to Christian life style;
transformationalist religious education (employed pejora-
tively here) looks for meaning and purpose in reflection
on experience which is denuded of the richness of inher-
itance. At the very least the present volume contributes to
a vision of religious education which is attentive to the
testimony of the past, the experience in the present and
the lure of the future. What the volume may be less attentive to is the ironic, even tragic character of the enterprise.
For finally, the fully dialectical practice of religious education is not achieveable; it functions as Reinhold Niebuhr's
"valuable illusion" which "in the task of redemption . . .
men have substituted . . . for the abandoned ones."[5]

And this is true by reason of the reality to which religion
refers, for religion is always "a vision of something that
stands beyond and within the passing flux of immediate
things; something which is real and yet waiting to be
realized; something which is a remote possibility and yet
the greatest of present facts; something that gives meaning
to all that passes and yet alludes apprehension; something
whose possession is the final good and yet is beyond all

reach; something which is the ultimate ideal and the hopeless quest."[6]

NOTES

1. Paul Tillich's language; see "Theology of Education," in *Theology and Culture,* (New York: Oxford University Press, 1964).
2. Langdon Gilkey, "New Modes of Empirical Theology," in B. Meland, ed., *The Future of Empirical Theology* (Chicago: Chicago University Press, 1969), p. 356. "Religious discourse has meaning only . . . as it thematizes ordinary secular experience, namely, the ranges of experience where ultimacy and sacrality are apprehended."
3. Jerome Bruner, *Toward a Theory of Instruction* (Cambridge: Harvard University Press, 1966), p. 128.
4. Padraic O'Hare, ed., *Foundations of Religious Education* (New York: Paulist Press, 1978). Contributors were Thomas H. Groome, James Michael Lee, Berard Marthaler, Gabriel Moran, and Francoise Darcy Berube.
5. Reinhold Niebuhr, *Moral Man and Immoral Society* (New York: Charles Scribner and Sons, 1932), p. 277.
6. Alfred North Whitehead, *Science and the Modern World* (New York: Macmillan, 1925), p. 142.

1

Access to Traditions and Transformation

Mary C. Boys, S.N.J.M.

A recent special section in *Time* magazine extols the development of "miracle chip" computers as a quantum leap in technology. The Industrial Revolution had merely expanded productivity by releasing humans from the limits of their physical capacity, but now miniscule and cheap computers are "rapidly assuming huge burdens of drudgery from the human brain," and thereby expanding the mind's capacity in ways not yet even comprehensible. Those members of the "electronic priesthood" involved in refining and marketing this quantum leap in technology thus proffer humankind "salvation in a world of crushing complexity."[1]

It is tempting to play with the number of religious terms appropriated in the description of the computers. It would furthermore be fascinating to delve into some of our own ambivalent reactions to such promises of near utopia as illustrative of the very duality of tradition and change which this symposium addresses. But, more directly to the issue at hand, could a computer help us to make sense out of the confusions and contradictions which presently abound in the as-yet-inadequately conceptualized disci-

pline called "religious education"? What if the assorted
definitions and descriptions that have accumulated over
the years were programmed and fed into a computer?

It is an intriguing thought and undoubtedly not out of
the realm of possibility. But for the present we have only
our human powers of analysis and insight to bring to
bear—powers which may provide less certainty than a
computer printout, but ultimately give more adequate
witness to the profound mystery of life.

Our purpose, as I understand it, is to dialogue about
what it is we are doing when we engage in religious education; more specifically, it is to address this foundational
question in terms of a definition of religious education
which holds in fruitful tension both the handing on of
traditions and the changing of the world.

I. TRADITIONS AND TRANSFORMATION

Computers, as the *Time* article reports, make sense out
of binary numbers by using three logical functions: "and,"
"or," and "not." Similarly, I will employ those functions in
order to describe what constitutes religious education.
Though I will argue later that "and" is the proper connec-
tive to describe how religious education stands amid the
polarities of conservation and change, continuity and
transformation, nurture and mission, I want first to situate
the problem in its classical "or" formulation.

Perhaps no one has laid out the polarity so starkly as
George Albert Coe: "Shall the primary purpose of Christian
education be to hand on a religion, *or* to create a new world?"[2]
Transmissive education, in Coe's view, encompassed the pol-
icies and practices grounded in the assumption that educa-

tion ought, above all, to perpetuate an already existing culture. Characteristically, it tended to employ either force or evasion in the interest of effectiveness, was preoccupied with content and resisted vigorous analysis of changing conditions. Creative education, on the other hand, rested on the premise that education primarily involved the reconstruction of society. Reconstruction constituted the essence of the divine in the human order.

Coe, as a disciple of the Social Gospel movement, a colleague of John Dewey and a fellow proponent of progressive education, was imbued with the social element. In 1917 he had argued that the aim of Christian education was *not* the instruction of children in things Christians ought to know, *not* to prepare them for church membership, *not* to save their souls, *not* to impose the truth, but to promote "growth of the young toward and into mature and efficient devotion to the democracy of God, and happy self-realization there."[3] He coined a phrase in that same work that offers a minor leitmotif for this paper: "We should never turn an adolescent over to *uneducational evangelism*" (emphasis added).[4]

This "uneducational evangelism" is precisely what Coe equated with transmissive education. In reaction to the nineteenth century "ecology" of institutions of Protestant religious education—tract societies, revivals, Sunday schools, missionary alliances, temperance unions—Coe transposed religious symbols into social and ethical imperatives.[5] As heir of the liberal theology of Adolf von Harnack, who had reduced Christianity to an essential core and denied the legitimacy of dogmatic meanings, Coe developed a religious system devoid of dogma or mysticism. Infatuated with empirical, scientific methods and filled with the immanentist, progressive spirit of the post-Darwinian epoch,

he castigated authoritarian systems. Salvation was by education; religious education dealt not with doctrine but with
growth and the transformation of values. As he defined
religious education:

> It is the systematic, critical examination and reconstruc-
> tion of relations between persons, guided by Jesus' as-
> sumption that persons are of infinite worth, and by the
> hypothesis of the existence of God, the great valuer of
> persons.[6]

Not surprisingly, then, Coe had little regard for Catholic
education which, in his view, perpetuated and made uni-
versal an autocratic government of religious and ethical
thinking and of religious and moral conduct. It was the
"very antipodes of the aspiration for a democracy of God";
it transmitted a completed faith and did not facilitate the
evolution of faith.[7]

For all the limitations of Coe's modernist standpoint, for
all the naiveté of a position which equated the kingdom of
God with industrial democracy, nonetheless one may, it
seems to me, grant a solid basis for his dichotomy of
transmissive versus creative education. The Catholicism,
for instance, that Coe saw was indeed preoccupied with
transmitting a "completed" faith. The reaction to the
modernist challenge at the turn of the century serves as
the most vivid example of this mentality; the Baltimore
Catechism exists as the most enduring symbol of this trun-
cated way of "handing on the faith."[8] Only against this
context, in fact, can one appreciate the power of Austrian
Jesuit Josef Jungmann's 1936 critique:

> . . . Religious teaching today cannot content itself with
> the mere handing on of hereditary formulas, nor can it

assume, as it once did, that the traditional sum of customs, devotions, pious thoughts and practices, even intensively used, will avail to hold the faithful firmly in the Church and assure security and nourishment for their religious life. Today religious teaching must lead the faithful to a vital understanding of the content of faith itself, that they may interiorly grasp it, and thus grow to spiritual maturity and proper independence in religious life.[9]

Jungmann's proposals, which inaugurated the "kerygmatic renewal" (associated particularly with the idea of "salvation history") characteristic of Catholic religious education in the United States in the 1960s, seem from the present point of view almost passé, or at least far from revolutionary. The cataclysmic nature of his work is more apparent when one realizes that *Die Frohbotschaft* was "withdrawn" from circulation by request of the Holy Office and permission to translate it into English denied.[10]

Coe and Jungmann, both opposed to a mindless transmission of ready-made formulas of faith, nevertheless had fundamental differences. But the point I wish to establish in bringing them together is that, historically, there is a warrant for speaking of religious education that "hands on" traditions as the *antithesis* of religious education that "changes the world." Unless the logic of the polarity is seen, it will not be possible to hold the two in dialectical tension as I shall now propose.

Having thereby justified the usage of "or," I want now to argue that "and" is the more proper connection between handing on traditions and changing the world. Traditions, as history indicates, may become absolutized and without vitality. On the other hand, preoccupation with changing

the world may easily degenerate into an uncritical exalta-
tion of the present moment and into nonreflective
practice. I can think of no more marvelous description
than that of Francine du Plessix Gray, who designates educational relevance as the "Women's Wear Daily of reality, a
hem-like notion that changes every year according to the
fluctuating stamina of educators."[11] Relevance, as George
Tavard notes, is but the "surface texture of thought."[12]

If religious education is to avoid the pitfalls of fossiliza-
tion and an uncritical pursuit of relevance, then it must
both serve *and* change, continue ancient symbols *and* explore new possibilities, hand on traditions *and* transform
the world. Traditions, like roots, are lifelines to vital
sources from which new entities develop. Tradition exists
to make transformation possible.

Transmission and creation, paradoxically, must be held
in tension. Religious education needs to find a way not
only to affirm that both are true, but to incorporate both
poles in its theory and practice. It is that task to which we
turn in the next section.

II. Religious Education as Making Accessible

In the preceding section, the conjunctions "or" and
"and" served to highlight the problem; in this one, it is the
verbs which will focus attention on the solution. To put it
simply, which verb best expresses what it is we are about
when we engage in religious education: preach? proclaim?
evangelize? socialize? indoctrinate? develop? be with? instruct? reconstruct? make accessible? How do these verbs
govern the way we educate religiously?

Many of these verbs express mutually compatible activities, though it should be obvious, for example, that the choice of "reconstruct" à la Coe would necessarily preclude "indoctrinate." Many religious educators would choose a combination of these verbs and organize them into a hierarchy expressive of the varying modes of their activity and the relative significance of each. A caveat, however, lest one too eagerly choose from a verbal smorgasboard: eclecticism may hinder systematic analysis.

Perhaps the best way to avoid this mélange is to select a verb which allows for both transmission and transformation, nurture and mission. My claim is that "make accessible" is the verb which ought to function as the primary description of religious education.

Accessibility is best seen in its examplars: erecting bridges, making metaphors, building highways, providing introductions and commentaries, translating foreign terms, mapmaking and ice-breaking (literally and figuratively) are all instances. Destruction is also an exemplar; it offers a way of removing obstacles. Demolition experts, for instance, use radical means in a controlled fashion as the initial step in providing access.

Each of the disciplines is, in a sense, a way of access. History provides a coherent pattern amid the accumulated data of the past, biology a means by which the intricacies of living things are grasped, and art a way of entering into the imagination of the human spirit. In Christian theology, Jesus is frequently viewed as providing ultimate access to God—"I am the way, and the truth and the life" (John 14:6)—and his early disciples identified themselves as followers of the "way" (Acts 9:2; 19:9, 23; 22:4; 24:14, 22).

To what do religious educators give access? To the polarities: traditions and transformation.

III. Access to Traditions

To speak of religious education as the making accessible of traditions is not so anachronistic as it may initially appear. Tradition is memory; without it humankind would be incapable not only of personal relationships but also of building a civilization. "Tradition! Tradition! A man without tradition is as shaky as a fiddler on a roof!"

While in some respects contemporary culture seems to dismiss the significance of tradition, from other standpoints contemporary theology and philosophy provide exciting possibilities for reconsidering the meaning.

Biblical theology offers one of the most vital analogues for redeeming the term. In OT studies, for instance, much discussion centers on how Israel's faith came to expression through a long and complex process of development; how memories precious to one region (Jerusalem, Bethel, Shechem) or group (priests, wise men, Levites, prophets, court officials) were shaped, applied and passed on; and how these "streams of tradition" ultimately flowed together to form a sacred literature.

The applicability of this "tradition history" to religious education struck me only last year as I was rereading Gerhard von Rad's magnum opus, *Old Testament Theology*.[13] This brilliant piece of scholarship obviously cannot be summarized adequately here, but perhaps several examples will highlight the analogy. Von Rad characterizes the prophets as those who "reactualized" (*vergegenwärtigen*) the ancient traditions by selecting, combining, and rejecting various components of tradition. He shows, for instance, how the "salvation oracle" (with the formula "do not fear"; see Is 41:8-13, 14-16; 43:1-3a, 5; 44:2-5; 49:7, 14-15; 51:7-8; and 54:4-8) which assured Israel of

Yahweh's nearness was actually a derivation from, and a reversal of, certain laments. Well known is the lament of the psalmist (22:6), "But I am a worm and no man," which Second-Isaiah transposes into a word of assurance, "Fear not, you worm Jacob" (Is 41:14).[14]

Similarly, Second Isaiah drew freely upon the tradition of the exodus to encourage the exiles. This was in actuality a very bold reactualization: the prophet appropriates the language descriptive of Israel's most sacred event to give hope in the midst of what appeared to be the greatest tragedy the people had experienced.[15]

A rereading of Isaiah 40–55 will immediately make von Rad's point evident; throughout are images of deliverance, of God leading his people, revealing himself in the wilderness and so on. But note particularly the prophet's contrast between "former things" (43:18) and "new things" (43:19; 48:6b): what has happened in the past (the exodus) is but a prelude to what will happen in the future. Isaiah is not merely using old traditions for the sake of reverencing antiquity, but "reactualizing" them for the sake of what they reveal about present and future when transposed into a new key. To speak of the return from exile as a new exodus is to make a bold claim!

The traditions of Israel, as von Rad vividly describes, are not a series of hard and fast rules, but living memories which *narrate*, *instruct*, *regulate*, *inform*, and *interpret* the experience of Israel.[16]

Jesus, too, recognized the diversity of traditions. Some he judged unacceptable because they did not witness to the kind of kingdom he envisioned: "How well you set aside the commandment of God in order to maintain your tradition!" (Mark 7:9; cf. Mark 7:1, 15). Some traditions Jesus reinterpreted: "You have learned that our forefathers were told. . . . But what I tell you is this . . ." (Matt 5:21, 27, 33, 38, 43). Others he appropriated more in the mainstream of Jewish tradition (on the greatest commandment, Mark 12:29 and par.), or in a fashion similar to the traditions of Essene (such as in his *pesher* ["this is that" fulfillment motif] exegesis, e.g. the usage of Is 61:1–2 in Luke 4:16–20).

The methodologies of form and redaction criticism seek to account for the way the materials of the Christian tradition were preserved, interpreted, and modified. As with their sister endeavors in OT studies, they represent tentative and, at times, hypothetical reconstructions. But the conjectural aspects of form and redaction criticism need not obscure their fundamental portrayal of the primitive church as a spirit-filled group of men and women who remembered the words and deeds of Jesus in such a way that their memories both shaped and were shaped by the exigencies of daily life.

To study the NT with the tools of biblical criticism, for instance, is to discover that even the words of Jesus were not regarded as static. Note that form critical studies isolate two sayings on divorce attributable to Jesus himself (the pronouncement in Mark 10:9 and its par. in Matt 19:6; the dominical saying in Luke 16:18a–b), and that redaction criticism makes manifest the developments of that tradition in the additional Markan material (10:12a–b), exceptive phrases in Matt (5:32b; 19:9b) and the Pauline recension from a woman's standpoint (1 Cor 7:10c).[17] A less complex but similar example is the parable of the sower and the seed (Mark 4:3–9 and par.), to which the early church has added its allegorical catechesis (Mark 4:13–20).

Obviously this is not the forum to engage in an apologia

for historical-critical methods in scripture study. But what I am concerned to demonstrate is that the tools of criticism provide us with insight into the fascinating and complex process by which the traditions of the Jewish and Christian communities were remembered and reactualized. They offer us a perspective on the malleability and vitality of traditions. Furthermore, tradition and redaction criticism provide a view of the various interests which catalyzed the preservation and adaptation of traditions, why, for instance, Matthew is concerned to make an exception (Matt 5:32b "except for unchastity" [RSV]) to the prohibition of divorce for Gentile Christians who lived among Jewish Christians still observing Mosaic regulations.

Tradition, then, provided the very "stuff" out of which new was drawn from old (see Matt 13:51). It was made accessible in ever creative and diverse ways. Let there be no doubt that what was handed on was done with care lest the living nature of tradition be lost. As Klaus Koch has remarked: "The biblical word has proved to be not truth in a fossilized, unchanging sense, but truth which is constantly adapting itself to the circumstances of the time."[18]

Contemporary biblical scholarship has thus served as my prime exemplar in reevaluating the place of tradition in religious education. I regard C. Ellis Nelson's book, *Where Faith Begins*, as offering a substantially similar understanding, and as a model of clarity and insight.[19] Moreover, I believe that refinements in biblical scholarship since the publication of that work now make it possible to see that an understanding of tradition gives religious education a basis not only in the literature of socialization but also facilitates the application of the sociology of knowledge and of critical theology.

In short, an understanding of the process of gospel

composition enhances the very notion of reconstruction
that Coe thought to be incompatible with tradition. Moreover, modern biblical scholarship contradicts the mentality
of a "blueprint ecclesiology" in which it is presumed Jesus
specified and insured a detailed plan for the church.[20]
Thus it reveals the inadequacies of any schema which di-
vorces transmission from re-creation, whether that be a
"liberal" schema, such as Coe's, or a "conservative" one,
such as that of Jungmann's opponents.

It therefore may be appropriate to revise an understanding of the term "deposit of faith." I must confess that,
until recently, I considered this an unfortunate metaphor
which imaged neatly packaged truths piled one upon the
other. But an examination of the etymology suggests reconsideration: "deposit" stems from the neuter past parti-
ciple, *dēpositum*, of the Latin verb, *dēpōnere*, and means
"that which is laid down." Furthermore, the infinitive
means not only "to lay down," but also, "to testify."

To conceptualize the "deposit of faith" as our heritage
or ground of *testimonies* suggests the dialogical element
inherent in the passing on of traditions. To make tradition
accessible is to open up the past, rather than to set it aside
as "other." It is to let the past speak in the present for the
sake of the future; it is not, on the contrary, to dictate past
answers for present problems. The "deposit of faith" refers to the living tradition with which we are entrusted. It
is, as Gadamer says of tradition, a genuine partner in
communication with which we have fellowship as does the
"I" with a "thou."[21]

George Tavard provides a similarly vital view of tradition by describing it as the "living and lived self-
consciousness of the thinking members of the church," as
the "memory of the community," as the "permanent reser-

voir of pieces for construction and reconstruction," as the *sensus ecclesiae*.[22] It emerges out of a process in which believers interpret the memory of the past as normative for the faith of the future: the past becomes tradition insofar as it is shaped by the anticipated future. Thus tradition is never final, never fixed; it changes as believers receive it differently in light of the future. In other words, it is modified by praxis.[23]

Implicit in Tavard's thought is the paradox suggested by Langdon Gilkey: in order to reach authentic tradition, one must begin anew.[24] Or to put it in another way, believers are not being faithful to tradition when they merely repeat ancient formulas (even if they are biblical sayings) or enshrine them in timeless abstractions.[25] Hence, indoctrination is incompatible with fidelity to tradition. "Uneducational evangelism," to use Coe's phrase, is actually insufficiently traditional!

The unfinished nature of tradition means that the church is not only teacher but also learner. Religious education thus refers to the mutuality of education in faith; it means that the mystic learns from the child, the scholar from the unlettered, the teacher from the student.

This, however, involves some difficult political ramifications. In Roman Catholicism, for example, the view has gradually evolved that the teaching office belongs to the papacy and episcopacy alone; already by the third century, the principle seemed established that instruction in the faith properly devolved upon the clergy under the guidance of the bishop. That principle contrasted with the situation of the apostolic era in which teachers had authority by virtue of their knowledge rather than by connection with the episcopacy.[16] Neoscholasticism served to reinforce and legitimate the equation of the charism of teaching with episcopal office. As a consequence, teaching has often been viewed more juridically than charismatically.

As a corrective to the juridicizing of the teaching office, Avery Dulles suggests an alternative model of two complementary and mutually corrective magisteria: pastors and theologians.[27] This suggestion is grounded in the Thomistic distinction between the "magisterium of the pastoral or episcopal chair" and the "magisterium of the teaching chair," and is, in Dulles's view, both more representative of Catholic tradition and the NT understanding of the charism of the *didaskaloi* (teachers).

In light of this, I propose that the legitimacy of religious education as an endeavor in its own right be acknowledged. Religious education is not merely a popularization of, nor a delivery system for, theology or ecclesiastical teachings. Rather, it is a configuration of disciplines with its own coherence (or at least in search of it), concerned with making the traditions of religious communities accessible in all their vitality, diversity, and specificity. Thus it may need to "demolish" sterile traditions, "re-mediate" those overgrown with accretions, and "provide introduction" to traditions overlooked in a preoccupation with relevance. Religious education, furthermore, would seem in this era to have a special mediational function; it may well be the most fitting enterprise capable of "erecting bridges" between theologian and pastor, pastor and people, theologian and people, theologian and educator, and so forth. Thus religious educators need to speak both ecclesiastical and educational languages.[28]

By so doing, I believe that religious education will both hand on a religion and create a new world; to hand on traditions is in fact to recreate and to reconstruct. The re-creative element of religious education will be the focus of the following section.

IV. ACCESS TO TRANSFORMATION

Mindful that an ahistorical and insufficiently nuanced understanding of tradition (which I prefer to call "traditionalism") may lead to an authoritarian and desiccated mode of religious education, I am nevertheless arguing for the significance of an expanded notion of tradition. Tradition, from my perspective, is the very foundation of religious education.

The full dimensions of this are seen by reflecting on the complementary foundational element, transformation. What does it mean for religious educators to give access to transformation?

It means, above all, the acknowledgment that tradition is to be acted upon. The history of Israel and of the early church are paradigmatic in this respect: traditions were reactualized for the sake of living a relationship with God and neighbor. The stories and sayings passed on from generation to generation were not for entertainment but for the edification (in its literal sense of "building") of the community. Traditions, derived from living, provided the reflective basis for action. Practice, in turn, shaped the preservation of tradition.

One of the best known features of Semitic anthropology is that it does not separate knowing from doing, or feeling from willing. The verb *yādâ,* "to know," refers not merely to cognitive comprehension but to intimate experience, and is used in some cases to refer to sexual intercourse. Likewise, *leb,* "heart," encompasses characteristics that

Western thought has more generally ascribed to the mind (reason, insight, memory, perception, knowledge, judgment, discernment); the heart is the place of decision, the organ symbolic of understanding and will. To be given a new heart (Ez 36:26) is to be given new insight and will for change.[29]

Now there is always possibility of distortion when one takes words out of context.[30] My point, however, is not to engage in an extended theological treatise on biblical vocabulary but to make evident that there is an essential unity in the Jewish and Christian traditions. To know the Lord is to do the Lord's will. To be granted a heart renewed is to be graced with the possibility of living differently.

This is by no means an original insight and undoubtedly not a controversial one as long as it remains of the level of abstraction. The "rub" occurs in agreeing on the implications. That is, what does it actually mean in concrete, specific terms to know God's will and thereby to do it?

It is because of the immensity of this question that I prefer to speak of religious education as a means of access to transformation rather than as an actual means of transformation. The distinction is grounded in the realization that divine grace and human freedom must be honored above all else. Religious education begins in awe.

Admittedly, this is a subtle distinction, lest the essential unity between tradition and transformation be obscured. I am not suggesting that religious education avoid either pressing crucial questions of significance or probing for the ethical and political ramifications of the traditions. Christians, for instance, cannot project the "glad tidings" of the gospel into an other-worldly happiness, or they have missed the meaning of the incarnation. If God saw fit to "pitch his tent" in the ordinary, workaday world, Christian religious educators can hardly do otherwise.

But, on the other hand, they must submit their own visions and convictions to what I call an "asceticism of negativism," a process of continual questioning of presuppositions and standpoints. It may be just as idolatrous to equate the diversity of traditions with any single economic or social system as it is to worship a God who makes no demands.[31]

Religious education as a means of access to transformation may be better understood if some of the pedagogical implications are examined. As a general principle, it seems imperative to observe that styles of teaching which continually reinforce what Freire terms "banking education" are at variance with both the vitality of traditions and with the freedom of religious transformation.[32]

Perhaps two illustrations of alternative pedagogies will provide food for further thought. The first is an account by journalist Paul Cowan of his reclamation of the Jewish tradition through the religious education of his children.[33] Having been raised in a secularized Jewish home, he felt nonetheless a strong sense of pride in his Judaism and a desire to experience a direct and personal connection to his heritage. Knowing little about the traditions, he sought out, along with others in a similar dilemma, help from the New York Havurah, an organization of well-educated Jews anxious to reexamine their faith. Four of the Havurah members set up a school (an "open corridor 'cheder'") which met once a week and which involved the parents as much the children. For instance, as Cowan reported:

> It is all very carefully planned. Each week the teachers meet for four to six hours to prepare for every two hour

class. And the parents and teachers spend an evening
together every two weeks, often to discuss how the major episodes in Genesis and Exodus should be presented. That means we have to evaluate our own feelings
about Abraham's willingness to sacrifice Isaac, or the
cunning Jacob displayed toward Esau. So we end up
studying the Torah, too. It is the first time some of us
have done that.[34]

Several points of significance may be highlighted. First,
note the mutuality of the relationships: the Havurah
members are rethinking their faith by their involvement
with those less familiar with Judaism, the questions of the
children are leading their parents to ask their own questions, and the parents' questions are shaping the pedagogy
of their children. Secondly, the article (of which only a
brief citation has been given) evidences the care and
creativity with which the Havurah members sought to represent the Jewish traditions to the initiates; I doubt they
could do this if they themselves were not in the midst of
their own processes of reconstruction. Thirdly, Cowan
mentions the way community has been built up and the
way individual members have manifested their concern
for one another; implicitly, this speaks of a concern for
transforming lives.

The second illustration is the parabolic pedagogy of
Jesus. What might it mean to teach as Jesus did?

The parables, contrary to popular understanding, are
not homely little comparisons designed to make their
hearers comfortable with God's word. To the contrary,
they represent what David Tracy, drawing upon Paul
Ricoeur, calls the "limit vision" of human possibilities.[35]

They interweave realism and strangeness. Dominic Crossan calls them "raids on the articulate,"[36] stories whose artistic surface structure allows them to invade a person's hearing in direct contradiction to the deep structure of his or her expectations. It is not the hearer who interprets the parable, but the parable which interprets the hearer.

Thus, as Sally TeSelle writes in her excellent book, *Speaking in Parables*, listeners are summoned to "imaginative participation."[37] Parables are less moral fables than calls to decision, less pious examples than metaphors of the kingdom. The parable of the Good Samaritan, for instance (Luke 10:30–37), is not a moral about helping neighbors who are "down and out." Rather, it is a shocking narrative about how the least in God's kingdom—in this case, the hated Samaritan—is in fact the greatest.

Parables, as part of tradition, are perpetually unfinished. As Robert Funk suggests, "the parable opens onto an unfinished world because that world is in course of conception."[38] They are imaginative and suggestive rather than didactic and prescriptive.

Jesus is the storyteller par excellence. His parables tease, surprise, and confront. But he calls for decision from his hearers in such a way that those who have "ears to hear" are left to wrestle with the meaning of that decision for their lives. The parabolic pedagogy of Jesus is a paradigm of freedom in religious education. It suggests that his followers develop what literary critic Northrop Frye has entitled one of his books, *The Educated Imagination*, so that they can live the ordinary in a new way.[39] An educated imagination is an opening to transformation. "To picture to oneself" (*imāginārī*) is to enter into the dialogue that is tradition.

V. THREE MODES OF TRADITION AND
TRANSFORMATION

Finally, it may be helpful to consider religious education as making accessible traditions and the means to transformation according to three interrelated modes.

The first, the proclamatory (implying religious education as preaching, proclaiming, evangelizing), mirrors the catechesis of Israel and the early church. Both the OT and NT include brief *credenda* or kerygmatic statements heralding God's "mighty acts."[40] Such proclamation is a significant moment in the process of educating religiously, but is far too limited a concept to deal with the complexity and malleability of traditions. Furthermore, excessive emphasis on the proclamatory mode can lead to an equation of teaching with telling. It is not enough to announce the good news; if the good news is told in such a fashion as to imply that everything is thereby settled, it is "uneducational evangelism."

Narration is a second mode of religious education. In scripture the proclamatory statements were "filled in" by vivid stories; so also in religious education, the fundamental faith claims need to be filled in and explored. Here neophyte and teacher are mutually immersed in the stories and symbols constitutive of their religious identity. Narrative represents the fundamental shape of the datum to which neophytes are introduced, and is the mode of socialization. Because, as the parables so well illustrate, believing has a narrative quality, this mode holds great promise. I also see it as integrally linked to a third mode, interpretation.

Interpretation is the critical distance the hearers put between themselves and the narrative so as to determine the implications. It encompasses what is called "formation of conscience" and respects the mystery of divine grace and human freedom. Paul Ricoeur has captured its two movements under the rubric of a "hermeneutic of suspicion" and a "hermeneutic of restoration," and much benefit could be derived from attention to the pedagogical implications of those dual interpretative moments.[41] What, for instance, is the shape of teaching strategies that can build critical inquiry and facilitate reconstruction? Such a question, I believe, would provide a challenging agenda for teacher education.

To proclaim, to narrate, to interpret: these are three fundamental ways of giving access to traditions and the means to transformation. Their relationship to one another bears further study, and needs especially to be informed by developmental theory. The relative importance assigned to each mode should be determined by the manner in which they make accessible, and then the other verbs descriptive of corollary activities (evangelize, socialize, etc.) arranged accordingly.

VI. CONCLUSION

The editors of *Time* are right: we do live in a world of "crushing complexity." If I am less confident than they that "miracle chip" computers can provide salvation, I have little doubt that they can indeed provide immense breakthroughs for the retrieval of information and for greater ease in everyday living.

But no computer can, at least in my purview, ever adequately conceptualize religious education. Religious education reflects the complexity, ambiguity, and mystery of the relationship of divine and human, and is, hence, beyond the ken of computer technology.

What computers cannot solve, we must ourselves confront. I have myself been drawn to a reconsideration of religious education through study of the process by which scripture came to be; ancient writ lies open for endless understanding and is far more pertinent than computer analysis.

Using scripture as my principal exemplar, I maintain that religious education must necessarily be concerned with both traditions *and* transformation. I find Coe's polarity between transmission and reconstruction ultimately to be a false dichotomy, and argue that a deepened understanding of tradition is the key in holding both in tension.

Finally, I suggest that reflection on religious education as the making accessible of the traditions of religious communities and the means for their transformation is to speak not of a "quantum leap of technology," but of a way of renewing the face of the earth.

NOTES

1. "The Computer Society," *Time* 111 (February 20, 1978), pp. 44-59.
2. *What Is Christian Education?* (New York: Scribner's, 1930), p. 28. Emphasis added.
3. *A Social Theory of Religious Education* (New York: Scribner's, 1917), p. 55.
4. Ibid, pp. 182-183.
5. See H. A. Archibald, "George Albert Coe: Theorist for Religious Education in the Twentieth Century" (Ph.D. Dissertation, University of Illinois at Urbana-Champaign, 1975), p. 235.
6. *What Is Christian Education?* p. 296.

7. *A Social Theory of Religious Education*, p. 298. See Archibald, pp. 225 and 260. Cf. Coe's views with Catholic philosopher Orestes Brownson who wrote in 1862: "The fault we find with modern Catholic education is not that it does not faithfully preserve the symbol, that it does not retain all the dogmas or mysteries, so far as sound words go, but that it treats them as isolated or dead facts, not as living principles, and overlooks the fact that the life of the church consists in their continuous evolution and progressive development and actualization in the life of society and of individuals." Cited in N. G. McCluskey, ed., *Catholic Education in America: A Documentary History* (New York: Teachers College Press, 1964), pp. 105–106.

8. On Coe as a Modernist, see W. R. Hutchison, *The Modernist Impulse in American Protestantism* (Cambridge: Harvard University, 1976), pp. 156–164. On the Modernist challenge in Catholicism, see T. M. Schoof, *A Survey of Catholic Theology 1800–1970* (New York: Paulist-Newman, 1970), pp. 14–156.

9. Originally published in *Die Frohbotschaft und unsere Glaubensverkündigung* and finally appearing in an abridged English translation as *The Good News Yesterday and Today,* eds. W. A. Huesman and J. Hofinger (New York: Sadlier, 1962), p. 7.

10. See Hofinger's account, "J. A. Jungmann (1889–1975): In Memorian," *Living Light* 13 (1976), pp. 354–356. See G. Diekmann's review (*Orate Fratres* 11 [1937], p. 142) and the story of the request for English translation (J. Hall, "The American Liturgical Movement: The Early Years," *Worship* 50 [1976]), p. 483.

11. "For Lycidas Is Dead," *New York Times Book Review* (June 19, 1977), p. 38.

12. "Tradition in Theology: A Methodological Approach," J. F. Kelly, ed., *Perspectives on Scripture and Tradition* (Notre Dame, In.: Fides, 1976), p. 107.

13. 2 vols. (New York: Harper and Row, 1957 and 1965).

14. *Old Testament Theology* 2, p. 241.

15. Ibid, p. 246: "In referring as he does to the new exodus, Deutero-Isaiah puts a question mark against 'Israel's original confession'; indeed, he uses every possible means to persuade

his contemporaries to look away from that event which so far had been the basis of their faith, and to put their faith in the new and greater one."

16. See D. A. Knight, *Rediscovering the Traditions of Israel*, rev. ed. SBL Dissertation Series no. 9 (Missoula, Mt.: Scholars Press, 1975), pp. 5–32. Also W. E. Rast, *Tradition History and the Old Testament* (Philadelphia: Fortress, 1972).

17. See J. A. Fitzmyer, "Matthean Divorce Texts," *Theological Studies* 37 (1976), pp. 197–226.

18. *The Growth of the Biblical Tradition: The Form Critical Method* (New York: Scribner's 1969), p. 100.

19. Atlanta: John Knox, 1967. Note particularly the third chapter, "The Dynamics of Religious Tradition"; here Nelson's thesis is that the socialization process operates within religious tradition and efforts to communicate the Christian faith should appropriate this. Another perspective is offered by M. Hellwig (*Tradition: The Catholic Story Today* [Dayton: Pflaum, 1974] 61), who speaks of religious education as the "process of tradition formalized and made self-conscious."

20. On modern biblical scholarship as a corrective to "blueprint ecclesiology," see R. E. Brown ("Difficulties in Using the New Testament in American Catholic Discussions," *Louvain Studies* 6 [1976], pp. 144–158. A "blueprint ecclesiology" is implicit in an understanding of tradition manifested by J. Daniélou (*The Lord of History* [Chicago: H. Regnery, 1958], pp. 7–8) who claims: "History before Christ was a preparation and an awaiting. Once he is come, the essential business is to hand on (παραδοσις [paradosis, "tradition"]) the sacred and now immutable trust delivered once and for all."

21. H.-G. Gadamer, *Truth and Method* (New York: Seabury, 1975). For an important perspective on Gadamer, his debate with critical theorist Jürgen Habermas, and the implications for Christian theology, see E. Schillebeeckx (*The Understanding of Faith* [New York: Seabury, 1974], pp. 55–77 and 102–155.

22. "Tradition in Theology: A Methodological Approach," pp.

118–122. See Tavard's other essay in the same volume, "Tradition in Theology: A Problematic Approach," pp. 84–104.
23. Ibid, 114. Cf. G. Moran (*The Present Revelation* [New York: Herder and Herder, 1972], p. 126), ". . . We are constantly engaged in 'revisionism' at the individual, national, international, and cosmic levels. So long as there is a future, the past will always be changing in meaning."
24. *Catholicism Confronts Modernity* (New York: Seabury, 1975), p. 30.
25. See G. Baum, *Faith and Doctrine* (New York: Paulist-Newman, 1969), pp. 119–122.
26. See B. Cooke, *Ministry to Word and Sacraments* (Philadelphia: Fortress, 1976), pp. 61–63 and 210.
27. "The Theologian and the Magisterium," *Catholic Mind* 75 (1977), pp. 6–16. Cf. Y. Congar, "The Magisterium and Theologians: A Short History" *Theology Digest* 25 (1977), pp. 15–20; Cooke, p. 276.
28. See G. Moran, "Two Languages of Religious Education," *Living Light* 14 (1977), pp. 7–15.
29. See H. W. Wolff, *Anthropology of the Old Testament* (Philadelphia: Fortress, 1974).
30. In scripture studies James Barr has been sharply critical of theological concepts derived primarily from philology (*The Semantics of Biblical Language* [London: Oxford University, 1961]).
31. See A. Dulles, "The Meaning of Faith Considered in Relationship to Justice," in J. C. Haughey, ed., *The Faith That Does Justice* (New York: Paulist, 1977), pp. 10–46.
32. P. Freire, *Pedagogy of the Oppressed* (New York: Seabury, 1974). "Banking education" refers to education as an "act of depositing, in which the students are the depositories and the teacher is the depositor. Instead of communicating, the teacher issues communiqués and makes deposits which the students patiently receive, memorize, and repeat. . . . In the banking concept of education, knowledge is a gift bestowed by those who

consider themselves knowledgeable upon those whom they consider to know nothing" (p. 58).

33. "World of Our Children," *New York Times Magazine* (April 3, 1977), pp. 63–70.

34. Ibid, p. 66.

35. *Blessed Rage for Order* (New York: Seabury, 1975), pp. 126–131.

36. "The Good Samaritan: Towards a Generic Definition of Parable," in J. D. Crossan, ed., *Semeia* 1 (Missoula, Mt: Scholars Press, 1974), p. 98. See his *In Parables* (New York: Harper and Row, 1973).

37. Philadelphia: Fortress, 1975, p. 83.

38. "The Good Samaritan as Metaphor," *Semeia* 2, p. 76.

39. Bloomington, In: Indiana University, 1964.

40. Gerhard von Rad cites Dt 26:5b–9 as the oldest creed in the Hexateuch: "My father was a homeless Aramaean who went down to Egypt with a small company and lived there until they became a great, powerful, and numerous nation. But the Egyptians ill-treated us, humiliated us and imposed cruel slavery upon us. Then we cried to the Lord, the God of our fathers, for help, and he listened to us and saw our humiliation, our hardship and distress; and so the Lord brought us out of Egypt with a strong hand and outstretched arm, with terrifying deeds, and with signs and portents. He brought us to this place and gave us this land, a land flowing with milk and honey" (*The Problem of the Hexateuch and Other Essays* [New York: McGraw Hill, 1966], p. 2). One of the oldest credal formulas of the resurrection would be 1 Cor 15:3–5: "I delivered to you as of first importance that I also received, that Christ died for our sins in accordance with the scriptures, that he was buried, that he was raised on the third day in accordance with the scriptures and that he appeared to Cephas."

41. *Freud and Philosophy* (New Haven: Yale, 1970).

2

Word, Sacrament, Prophecy

Maria Harris

INTRODUCTION

During this century, one of the strong points of religious education as a profession has been its ability to draw from many fields. The insights of psychology, sociology, philosophy, and the arts have shaped and conditioned much of what religious educators do, while the subject matter of theology and education has formed much of the content. What has been far less apparent, however, and to my mind a loss, has been the near absence of reflection on what we do by using lenses drawn from our religious traditions. Although we speak easily of religious education as creative, of the need for students and teacher to be present to one another, of educational activity to be critically engaged in, and of accepting the possibility of failure, we are less likely to articulate or write of creation, incarnation, judgment, and sin as ways of knowing ourselves as religious educators, or ways of understanding our lives together. Although we appreciate group investigation, personal sources, information processing and behavior modification as models of teaching,[1] we too rarely view education with such metaphors as the Quaker "Meeting for Learning,"[2] the Phenix idea of transcendence as inter-

preter of education,[3] or the Buber notion of education as
the forming of the image of God.[4] In this paper, it is such a
theme that I wish to pursue.

My intention is to ask what distinctive contributions the
Christian churches bring, out of their own experience, to
the field of religious education, that field where the religious and the educational intersect. In doing so, I wish to
illustrate the conviction that certain traditions shape the
enterprise when the churches carry it on. This is because
educating others in ways that are religious, and being religious in ways that educate are dependent on the traditions
sedimented in the flesh and psyches of the people involved. Thus, the view of tradition I will take here is that it
is something communities embody in their life and activity
together. What is handed over is a life, not statements or
verbal formulas. This life is communicated in many ways:
by the socializing and educative processes of culture and
subculture; by the images of oneself learned by looking at
the self reflected in the wishes and eyes of others, especially family and community; in the images of oneself and
one's people assigned by the wider society; and by the
reflective looking within that consciously contributes to
self-identity. In the course of our lives, belonging in a
primitive sense gives way to awareness of ourselves as
sometimes distanced from, sometimes part of a larger
group, and then on to a deeper experience of belonging
that is a synthesis of both the primitive and carefully
reflected-upon understanding of self.[5] This process, in
time, grows into a sense of ownership of ways of looking at
the world that are shared not only with communities in the
present, but with communities that stretch deeply into
both the past and the future. This shared ownership of
ways of looking at the world, in relationship to a people

who have gone before us, and to a people who will succeed us, is what I understand to be tradition.[6]

Of the many traditions built into the lives of those in the Christian churches over the centuries, I want to select three: word, sacrament, and prophecy. For the last few centuries, the first, word, has been more commonly associated with Protestantism, especially in such phrases as "sola scriptura", and the second, sacrament, more commonly associated with Catholicism. (Of course, there are no hard and fast boundaries, and both Christian bodies rightly claim the two. In addition, I do not want to suggest that only Christian people may lay claim to word and sacrament.) The third, prophecy, is a reminder to both of their Jewish roots, and a corrective which ideally keeps these traditions open to novelty and revelation, and closed to the premature conclusion that all truth resides with any one tradition or any one age. I select these three because, to my mind, they are so closely tied to religious education. For the religious educator, word, sacrament, and prophecy become embodied in three gracious acts: the act of teaching, the act of hallowing, and the act of parable. Each of these, in turn, has both an educational and a religious dimension. For teaching, the educational dimension is in naming, and the religious is in journey; for hallowing, the educational dimension is in ordering, and the religious is in the sacramental; for parable, the educational dimension is in questioning, and the religious is in foolishness. As my part in this conversation about the enterprise of religious education, I want to offer one model, admittedly one among several, which helps illuminate the religious education venture. I will suggest that if one is a religious educator working out of the Christian tradition, one contributes to education, the growth and development of the

human, by teaching, by hallowing, and by parable. I hope
to show that choosing these three as points of departure
creates the possibility of overcoming the split between
handing on tradition and changing the world. For when
teaching, hallowing, and parable are genuine, the education itself may be recognized as religious, the tradition may
be acknowledged as formative of the activity and the world
may be viewed as open to re-creation.[7] What this might
look like in actual practice is the burden of this paper.

I. TEACHING

Some time ago, I asked my students to respond to the
question, "What is teaching?" in Haiku form. Bill Maroon
answered:

Teaching

We meet—awkwardly.
I invite you to walk.
I find you dancing.

The poem needs no further explanation; every teacher
knows what it means. Teaching can be an artistic form,
and when engaged in with grace and skill be an obviously
aesthetic activity. The teacher as artist, or more simply as
good teacher, is one who designs an environment in such a
way that others are put in touch with their own resources,
and the resources in the environment.[8] Central to this act
of designing is the teacher's involvement in speech, and
more specifically in naming. Out of the many activities of
the teacher, the one I want to select for comment here is
this act of naming.

From an educational perspective, the teacher is one who names. Although teacher is quite different in meaning from facilitator, guide, or therapist, roles which may be preconditional or ancillary, teacher is very close in meaning to "the one who names." I use the word, not in the sense of labeling, but in the sense of initiating the other into acquaintance with reality, of the kind Helen Keller once described in speaking of Anne Sullivan:

> She brought me my hat, and I knew I was going out into the warm sunshine. This thought, if a wordless sensation can be called a thought, made me hop and skip with pleasure. We walked down the path to the well house, attracted by the fragrance of the honey-suckle with which it was covered. Someone was drawing water and my teacher placed my hand under the spout. As the cool stream gushed over one hand she spelled into the other word *water*, first slowly, then rapidly. I stood still, my whole attention fixed upon the motions of her fingers. Suddenly I felt a misty consciousness as of something forgotten—a thrill of returning thought; and somehow the mystery of language was revealed to me. I knew then that w-a-t-e-r meant the wonderful cool something that was flowing over my hand. That living word awakened my soul, gave it light, hope, joy, set it free! There were barriers still, it is true, but barriers that could in time be swept away.[9]

The teacher's naming takes other forms however. Besides initiating and inviting, the teacher's naming takes the form of discriminating for people, especially in the clarification of perceptions.[10] It takes the form of political action in the naming of injustice, illustrated so well by Freire[11] and by those who assist others, especially the young, in naming oppression in their lives.[12] It is an intelligent naming, knowing those things closest to the heart, as Ashton-Warner did with her Maori children;[13] and it is a sophisticated naming, knowing that the activity of naming is a function of power:

> "When I use a word," Humpty-Dumpty said in a rather scornful tone, "it means just what I choose it to mean—neither more nor less."
>
> "The question is," said Alice, "whether you can make words mean so many different things."
>
> "The question is," said Humpty-Dumpty, "which is to be the master—that's all."[14]

Finally, the teacher as namer knows the *connections* of words, especially the connections between words and gesture, words and touch, and words and silence. Knowing such connections allows the teacher the wisdom of choosing the time, paraphrasing Eliot, to name and not to name, and the time to sit still, waiting on the readiness of the other.

Naming for the religious educator occurs in the context of journey: this is the religious setting or dimension of depth in the teaching act. If the teacher's speech has an integrity to it, if the naming has been accurate, then these words create the possibility of journey. This is to say they allow for the possibility of religious education to be companioned, and for the trust and willingness to join in movement toward the unknown, toward mystery. For a short time, the teacher becomes a mentor, a co-learner, one who travels with, and one who can alert those being educated to the characteristic of the journey: that it has stages, which we know from Erikson, Piaget, Fowler, Gilligan, Kohlberg; that it involves meeting wise old men and wise old women (and religious educators might do well to insure that the generations meet as the journey goes on); that it is in part an intellectual quest which involves periods of darkness and inevitable doubt.

> . . . We need to doubt and question . . . At this point the "religion of the head" becomes equally important with the "religion of the heart," and acts of the intellect, critical judgement, and inquiry into the meanings and purposes of the story and the ways by which the community of faith lives are essential. Serious study of the story, and engagement with historical, theological, and moral thinking about life become important. The despairs and doubts of the searching soul need to be affirmed and persons need to join others in the intellectual quest for understanding.[15]

The journey involves, to my mind, two great challenges, which need to be named: the challenge of holding on, sometimes till the arms ache and the back bends and sweat runs down the face; and its paradoxical complement: letting go, with the kind of intuitive leap, conditioned hunch, and creative hope that pushes back boundaries. Perhaps it is here that the teacher can share the stories of those who have done just this: from Martin Luther King's visionary declaration at Washington in 1963, "seeing the mountain," to Dag Hammarskjold's affirmation in the midst of darkness that at some point one takes the risk of saying "yes," not knowing to whom, to what, or how; to Jesus of Nazareth's crying out the familiar prayer all Jewish children were taught to say when going to sleep: "Father, into thy hands I commend my spirit."

For finally, the journey involves the acknowledgement and the naming of death, not only the physical death toward which the journey moves, but the death of child-hood, of dreams, of marriages, of institutions. Such issues of life and death are central concerns of those who would educate religiously, and they have a familiar undersong. Underlying them, and influencing them if one has been and is being shaped by the tradition of the Christian churches, is a particular understanding of word. To name, and to engage in journey is to be affected by *dabar*, a word that means speech, and a word that means activity; to be affected by the Pauline assertion that the Christ is the *yes* and *amen* in which God's promises are fulfilled (2 Cor 1:20); and to be affected by *logos,* a word that means a human being who has preceded us on the journey, and who is in some sense not only truth and life, but the way of the journey itself.

II. HALLOWING

To hallow is to set apart as holy; to sanctify; to conse-crate; to honor as being sacred; to revere. Its root is the same as that for wholeness, the Greek "kailo." It is notable that in Whitehead's famous definition, a religious educa-tion is one that inculcates not only duty, but *reverence*, the foundation of reverence being the perception that the present holds within itself "the complete sum of existence, backwards and forwards, that whole amplitude of time which is eternity."[16] I would argue that this act of hallow-ing, of reverence, is the second major act of the religious educator, and from a Christian perspective, is founded on sacrament. Its educational dimension is order; its religious dimension is the sacramental.

Educationally, the act of hallowing begins with *order*, the attempt to bring inner and outer harmony out of chaos, out of the unformed. Until recently, bureaucratic and/or mechanical forms of ordering have influenced educators very strongly. Classical bureaucratic qualities of control from the top, differentiation of function, qualification, and precision[17] have caused many to order in the sense of "rank order"—highest to lowest, best to worst, most valued to least important. This, in turn, is manifested in such areas as the sequencing of materials, separation of subjects, stating of behavioral objectives, and grading and classification of persons. We are all too familiar with such lists as:

MEN	GOD	ANIMAL
WOMEN	MAN	VEGETABLE
CHILDREN	NATURE	MINERAL

and such forms of ordering have been particularly evident in schools, whether these are conducted in the public sector or by the churches:

> The tendency of formal schooling to isolate children during a period of "preparation" for adulthood has produced a rigid system of age-grading which has as one effect a fractionation of the human career. This tends to hinder the development of meaningful relationships among generations and cultivates a fragmented, rather than continuous concept of self. The prevailing idea that children can learn only *from,* not with, adults and the forced submission of youth to the rule of adults amplifies the conflict between generations and encourages a posture of dependence, a sense of powerlessness that may carry over from youth to adulthood.[18]

What I wish to point out here is the enormous shift that has occurred recently in our sense of what it is to order, a shift due in large part to racial, feminist, and ecological movements. The feminist movement has recalled the need for humans to engage in mutuality, leading to the possibility of reciprocity which touches relationships such as educator-educatee, teacher-student, woman-man, child-adult. Ecological movements have highlighted the interdependence of all existing materials and systems; and the native American movement has recalled to us such prophecies as those of Chief Seattle:

> All things are connected like the blood which unites one family. All things are connected. Whatever befalls the earth befalls the children of the earth. The humans did not weave the web of life, they are merely strands in it. Whatever they do to the web, they do to themselves.[19]

The connectedness of time which Whitehead speaks of as the foundation of reverence also exists in the interconnectedness of material creation and, from this understanding of order, today's educator ideally works. In the preparation of educational activity, the need for integration becomes a constant criterion, interlocking systems are agreed upon as given, and sequencing moves back and forth from a center, rather than from a top. For the religious person, this center is one where the divine is at the core, in the midst, as the still point of the turning world. Among those studying together, the movement is toward mutuality, especially of sex, race, and age. Toward that which is studied and to be understood, the stance modeled is a touching with gentle fingers, a knowing that all things are to be honored as of value, and an awareness that what exists is, in the first place organically, as distinct from logically, joined.

I believe that for the religious educator, ordering occurs in the context of the sacramental; this is the dimension of depth in the act of hallowing. By sacramental, I mean the affirmation that physical, material, bodily reality has a spiritual dimension, and that the divine is revealed through buildings and bridges and earth and wine and human flesh.

> The range of the Christian sacramental imagination is not restricted to the seven traditional sacraments. It is capable of seeing in the whole cosmos and in all human relationships a kind of symbolic realization of God's covenant with humanity.[20]

Recognition of the sacramental as the religious aspect in hallowing could begin with attention to environment as a necessary component of the religious educator's work, with perhaps special emphasis on diversity of setting. The areas of human life most obviously open to the sacramental vision, where people engage with and are addressed by the material world, one another, and the divine, are those where people work, love, and pray as much as those where they study. Thus the sacramental is a dimension in religious education that can keep alive the recognition that education is not equal to schooling, and that religious education is not equal to church schooling. Some of the possibilities this sacramental understanding, or sacramental imagination could lead to are: 1) the alerting one another to the need to challenge and critique what is nonsacramental in the waste of material goods, the continued rape and exploitation of the earth by individuals and industry, the pornographic display and use of human bodies, especially those of children and women; and the pollution of air and lungs by the poisons of auto exhaust; 2) the investigation of the importance of *place* to the human being, which for educators might mean special care given to the physical settings in which people study, and deliberate choices made to design learning contexts more intentionally; 3) the hallowing of dailyness: cooking, cleaning, buying, selling, fixing machines, caring for children, in the affirmation of the religious significance of work; and 4) the educating towards touching as a hallowing activity, from the intimate touching of human sexuality, to the celebrative touching of worship where one handles words, ritual, bread and wine with the conviction: I am standing on holy ground; I am a participant in the act of hallowing.

Such issues are central concerns for those who would either educate religiously or be together religiously in ways that educate. Underlying them for those in the churches is the affirmation that the Christian churches, especially Catholicism, have kept alive: we are a people who draw meaning from sacramental imagination, a sacramental vision which is for us a traditional quality of consciousness:

> The power of sacraments and consequently the purpose of their existence is to be understood in terms of a *quality of consciousness* whose facilitation and development is their fundamental function. The consciousness in question is not simply a speculative awareness for purposes of interpretation . . . but a practical act. This quality of consciousness which is the fruit of self-transcendence does not remove one from the everyday world, but reveals in that world deeper and deeper dimensions of meaning.[21]

III. Parable

Strictly speaking, a parable is not an act, but neither, strictly speaking, back to the Greek "*ballein*," "to throw," to get at the active and verbal quality on the word. It is this notion I want to pick up in suggesting that the third gracious act of the religious educator, formed by the Christian churches, but stretching back to Jewish roots in prophecy, is the act of parable.

John Dominic Crossan's formulation in *The Dark Interval* gives rich insight into the meaning of parable. In Crossan's typology, myth establishes world, apologue defends world, narrative investigates world, satire attacks world, and parable subverts world.[22] A parable is a story calculated to show the limits of our myths, the flaws in our apologues, and shadowy places in our narratives. Like satire, parable reminds us of limit and confronts us with the frightening realization that things could, quite possibly, be completely other than they seem. According to Crossan, parables *give God room*.[23]

> The stories of Jesus (are) parables intended to shatter the structural security of the hearer's world and therein, and thereby, to render possible the kingdom of God, the act of appropriation in which God touches the human heart and consciousness is brought to final genuflection.[24]

When religious educators engage in parable, as with teaching and hallowing, there is both an educational and a religious dimension. I suggest that the activity of questioning is the educational side of parable, and that foolishness is its religious appearance.

Just as *ballein*, the root of parable, is to throw, the purpose of human questioning is to throw into possibility the idea that things can be more than, other than, or even the opposite of what they seem. Questioning carries within it a dialectic as well.

> It requires much effort to learn which questions should not be asked and which claims must not be entertained. What impairs our sight are habits of seeing as well as the mental concommitants of seeing. Our sight is suffused with knowing, instead of feeling painfully the lack of knowing what we see. The principle to be kept in mind is to know what we see rather than to see what we know.[25]

I would argue that any education that does not take questioning as a central task is quite simply, not genuine education. It is not at all surprising that asking questions in human life often ends in the death of the questioner. To probe, to puzzle, to ask why, to suggest that things might be done differently than they are are tremendous challenges to any established system. But the act of parable is one that pushes the educator to question, and at a level deeper than that of information. The educator, ideally, seeks to encourage others to be seekers, always asking of social, political, economic, and linguistic systems, "Must they be this way?" Indeed, the educator must also ask these questions of the churches. For the questioner, no institution, no policy, no human procedures can be idolized; the questioner's task is to see to that. And, if Crossan is correct that parable subverts world, and by subvert we mean destroy, ruin, undermine, overthrow or at the very least turn upside down, then for some, the questioning must rise out of prophecy.

A prophet is one who cannot remain indifferent, who must ask questions; a characteristic of which Heschel writes: "Perhaps this is the issue that frightens the prophets. A people may be dying without being aware of it; a people may be able to survive, yet refuse to make use of their ability."[26] Such absence of indifference is characteristic of prophetic questioning: prophets, certainly the biblical prophets, are persons called to question, who clearly have almost no choice; who question with attention to what others might deem trivialities and with luminous and frightening detail.[27] They are persons who are *informed*; and who appear to have the strong, sneaking suspicion that God may not want them to die in bed.

The religious dimension of parable is an ancient tradition in the Christian churches: foolishness. The New Testament is rich in allusions to it. Paul does not hesitate to speak of the foolishness of God (1 Cor 1:25), the foolishness of the cross (1 Cor 1:18), and of the choice of the foolish things of the world which put to shame the wise (1 Cor 1:27). Mary, in the Magnificat, recalls how God traditionally "scatters the proud . . . puts down the mighty . . . exalts the lowly . . . fills the hungry with good things and sends the rich away empty" (Luke 1:51–53). The ambiguity, the contrasting of opposites, the change in expectations, and the element of surprise are all signs of foolishness, and in the Christian scriptures, these are traditionally connected with the divine.

Just before Christmas last year, in an attempt to explore the impact of foolishness in religious education, I took part in a class on clowning led by one of my students. After a brief verbal explanation, where we were reminded of the nonverbal, symbolic, and nonrational aspects of the clown, and directed to do something intentionally foolish for the

Christ's sake, we dressed in baggy, castoff clothes brought
for the occasion, and applied the white mask of death over
which we traced the superimposed features of new life.
Then we left the safety of our classroom, in twos and
threes, risking the possibility of being foolish in the midst
of a serious academic day. Most of us chose to give away
money, food, fruit, and candy, and when that ran out, to
give away silent blessings. The children we met knew us
instantly (in Heschel's phrase, they "knew what they saw"),
as did the workmen, the Vice President for Development,
and several students and faculty we met on the way. But
there was no way of assessing our impact on others—that
had not been our intention—only of sharing the poig-
nancy, the silence, the newness, and the discovery with one
another. For that reason, it was peculiarly revelatory to
receive, two days later, a letter from an older student some
of the clowns had met and blessed, in traveling through
the administration building. The letter read:

Dear Wednesday Afternoon Fools:

Your smiling, funny faces
Found in unexpected places
Have brought a wondrous brightness to my day.
And the Tootsie Roll you gave me
Though it maybe didn't save me
It helped me one more step along the way.

The season here is lonely,
And I believe that only
Those who live it can relate to what I mean.
Every "blessed" thing is URGENT
Papers, finals, church-school pageant,
And the Advent/Christmas meaning leaves the scene.

But you came through a doorway,
And instead of blocking your way,
I received a tiny present that you found.
And your silent, clownish blessing
Has led me to confessing
That I went away with feet "on higher ground."

Marcia.

I use this story as a metaphor for the point I am trying to make with reference to all of life, but especially for religious educators. We may, in our own persons, have to be parables, people who subvert, who affirm ambiguity, who are able to reconcile opposites by taking risks. This is, indeed, a hallowed tradition, cited by Paul in reminding the Corinthians of the need to live dualities in their own persons: "in evil report and good report, as deceivers and yet truthful, as unknown and yet well known, as dying and behold, we live, as chastised but not killed, as sorrowful yet always rejoicing, as poor yet enriching many, as having nothing yet possessing all things" (2 Cor 6:8–10). But it is also a sign of prophecy, in a tradition much older than Paul, from which Paul drew: the willingness to speak forth in a way that seems deficient in understanding, sense or judgment; the decision to act unwisely in the presence of the great; and the choice to entertain risk in whatever form and at whatever time is necessary, whether that risk lies in retiring to a monastery, offending a patron, or protesting South African apartheid. Prophecy is at root based on the belief that God is inextricably involved in the lives of human beings, and that some of us are compelled to resist the institutional stabilizing of things, and by raising the question of meaning, make things uncertain and elastic in the process of history.[28] Prophecy is, finally, the reminder that all being is in question at the same time that all being may be the answering place where human and divine—greatest of parables—encounter one another.

OF CHRISTIAN RELIGIOUS EDUCATION, HANDING ON TRADITION, AND CHANGING THE WORLD

In conclusion, I wish to look at the title of this symposium and articulate how the foregoing pages are related to the three part issue we have been asked to address. I suspect it has been obvious throughout this paper that I have avoided the term Christian religious education, preferring to speak of the involvement of the Christian churches in religious education, or the participation by those formed by the Christian churches in religious education. Let me now come clean. I do not think it helpful to the field of religious education to add the term "Christian" before it. I hope it is clear that in my view, religious education is enriched as a field as all of us bring to it what is distinctly ours. But for my part, I would rather continue to ask how the religious and the educational intersect wherever they are found, than to invest energy in what is to me a more narrowly ecclesiastical and theological naming of what can only be a subfield. Trying to ask what is peculiar, to the purposes of Christian religious education, or indeed to invent a field that has this title remains for me an enterprise that is in danger of working from too isolated a context. I believe with Langdon Gilkey that Catholicism and Protestantism "must widen the scope of both word and sacrament far beyond their present religious, ecclesiastical, dogmatic, and merely redemptive limits,"[29] and that this principle must also extend to what has been called "Christian education" and "catechesis" as well. But I also wish to draw on the earlier comments made in this paper on the importance of naming. At present, Christian education is so synonomous with Protestant church education in this country, just as catechesis is with Catholicism, that I find it difficult to break through to new and more broadly ecumenical understandings of the field by using an unreconstructed language. Humpty-Dumpty's question is vividly pertinent at this point: Who *is* to be the master? For these reasons I prefer to stay with the term religious education.

With reference to handing on tradition, my intention in this paper has been to take word, sacrament, and prophecy, three familiar religious traditions, and illustrate how these might inform the enterprise of religious education. I do not wish to suggest that these are exclusive to the Christian churches. What I do wish to say, however, is that they are obviously present there, with prophecy being born in Judaism, and may be exemplars of the way tradition informs religious education. My hope would be that the model I have proposed would be just that, a model, and that others might return to their own traditions, or indeed to these three, and use them as points of departure for reflection as I have tried to do.

The issue of *what* is handed on, however, seems to me to be fairly clear. Drawing on the earlier comments made in this paper with reference to the connectedness of time and of created reality, what is handed on, in culture, in education, or in a church tradition, is the life of a people. Chesterton once remarked that tradition is the extension of the franchise to that most obscure of all classes, our ancestors. "It is the democracy of the dead. Tradition refuses to submit to the small and arrogant oligarchy of those who merely happen to be walking about."[30] In actuality, we who are the living do not so much receive the tradition; rather, we become the tradition, and each day of our lives makes this just a little more so.

Finally, to the question of whether our purpose is changing the world, I think yes, ultimately, that is our purpose. The end of all our exploring is a world that has been changed. Engagement in teaching, in hallowing and in parable are examples of ways one attempts to bring a changed world into being. But I would give nuance to my response by adding that it may not help to consciously articulate this purpose in day to day or year by year activity. In *Raise High the Roof Beam, Carpenters*, J. D. Salinger recounts the conversation between the young brother of Seymour and the twelve-year-old Seymour who has just won the marble playing championship of all Brooklyn. The young boy asks, "Seymour, what is the secret of your success?" Seymour remains silent for a while, thinking, and then answers: "Don't aim." I suspect much truth lies in that conversation—truth for us as religious educators. Aiming to change the world as one's daily task is a bit too grand, and probably a bit too overwhelming.

But what we might do, and what I have attempted to suggest in this paper, is engage in the kind of teaching, hallowing, and parable described here, with all the skill, devotion and *pietas* of which we are capable. This seems to me a more modest, more concrete, yet equally challenging formulation of the ideal, richly rooted in tradition. Being with others in ways that are both educational and religious can take such forms, although how they will come out remains shrouded in the mystery which human life is. Nonetheless, if we humans will attempt to understand from one another and grow in wisdom, speaking the word in truth; if we will accept and hallow the earth in the reverence born of sacrament; and if we will continue to stand forth and rage against inhumanity and injustice in human institutions and human culture, with the force and strength of prophecy, the world may indeed become different. The difference, however, will not merely be change; it will be the difference of re-creation.

NOTES

1. See Bruce Joyce and Marsha Weil, *Models of Teaching* (Englewood Cliffs: Prentice-Hall, 1972).
2. Parker J. Palmer, "How we Teach is More Important than What We Teach," in *Religion Teacher's Journal* (April, 1977), pp. 42, 44.
3. Philip Phenix, "Transcendence and the Curriculum," in Elliot Eisner and Elizabeth Vallance, eds., *Conflicting Conceptions of Curriculum* (Berkeley: McCutchan, 1974), pp. 117-132.
4. Martin Buber, *Between Man and Man* (New York: Macmillan, 1965), p. 102.
5. James W. Fowler, "Faith Development Theory and the Aims of Religious Socialization," in Gloria Durka and Joanmarie Smith, eds., *Emerging Issues in Religious Education* (New York: Paulist, 1976), pp. 187-211.
6. The American Heritage dictionary of the English Language defines tradition as 1. the passing down of elements of a culture from generation to generation, especially by oral communication; and 2. a mode of thought or behavior followed by a people continuously from generation to generation.
7. George Albert Coe asked the question this way: "Shall the primary purpose of Christian education be to hand on a religion or to create a new world?" See his *What is Christian Education* (New York: Scribner's, 1929), p. 29.

8. See Maria Harris, *The D.R.E. Book* (New York: Paulist, 1976), pp. 148–149.

9. Helen Keller, *The Story of my Life* (Garden City: Doubleday, 1936), pp. 23–24.

10. Gabriel Moran, *Religious Body* (New York: Seabury, 1974), pp. 162–166.

11. Paulo Freire, *Education for Critical Consciousness* (New York: Seabury, 1973).

12. John S. Mann, "Political Power and the High School Curriculum," in Eisner and Vallance, *Conflicting Conceptions*, pp. 147–153.

13. Sylvia Ashton-Warner, *Teacher* (New York: Simon and Schuster, 1963).

14. Lewis Carroll, *Through the Looking Glass* (New York: New American Library 1960. First published 1871), p. 186.

15. John Westerhoff, *Will Our Children Have Faith* (New York: Seabury, 1976), pp. 96–97.

16. Alfred North Whitehead, *The Aims of Education* (New York: Macmillan, 1929) p. 14.

17. Michael B. Katz, *Class, Bureaucracy and Schools: the Illusion of Educational Change in America* (New York: Praeger, 1971).

18. Fred M. Newmann and Donald W. Oliver, "Education and Community" in Theodore Sizer, ed., *Religion and Public Education* (New York: Houghton Mifflin, 1967), p. 199.

19. Patricia Mische, "Parenting in a Hungry World," in *New Catholic World* (Sept–Oct. 1977), p. 238, quotes this speech delivered in 1854, to mark the transferral of ancestral Indian lands to the federal government.

20. David Hollenbach, "A Prophetic Church and the Catholic Sacramental Imagination," in John C. Haughey, ed., *The Faith that Does Justice* (New York: Paulist, 1977), p. 253.

21. Joseph Powers, *Spirit and Sacrament* (New York: Seabury, 1973), p. 27.

22. (Niles: Argus, 1975).

24. Ibid., p. 123.

25. Abraham Heschel, *The Prophets* (New York: Harber and Row, 1962), p. xv.

26. Ibid., p. xvi.

27. Ibid., pp. 5-7.

28. Hollenbach, "A Prophetic Church," p. 242.

29. *In Catholicism Confronts Modernity: A Protestant View* (New York: Seabury, 1975), p. 197.

30. Gilbert K. Chesterton, *Orthodoxy* (Garden City: Image, 1959), p. 48.

3

Our Oldest Problem

C. Ellis Nelson

Christian education as a field of study and research is rather new; in America it began about 1900 and rapidly became important in our major universities and seminaries. Yet, after almost a century of research, some of the major problems remain unsolved.

Perhaps the oldest problem is the theme of this symposium: how can we transmit religion to the next generation without religion becoming merely a set of dogmatic beliefs? Or, how can adults live and teach their most cherished beliefs in such a way that children learn to relate to God and not to their parents' belief about God?

Asked this way, the question is seen as the educational component of a persistent life situation within the Judeo-Christian religion. From the earliest record of the history of Israel until the last New Testament book dealing with the church, we have a struggle between the revelations of God and religious traditions. While Moses was on the mountain composing the Ten Commandments, the people under Aaron's leadership made a calf from their golden rings in order to worship as they had done traditionally (Exodus 32). The letters of James, Peter, and John are among the latest books of the New Testament; and in them we find tension between those who want to live by the theological formulations of the past and traditional ways of worship. Between Moses and James, there are about fifteen hundred years of history in which this conflict had persisted. Thus, we have a Bible full of illustrations of how this tension comes about and what happens when one side or the other is dominant. In my book *Where Faith Begins*, I pointed out that the Bible describes a community of believers which carried along its life and literature a variety of beliefs. These beliefs were often challenged by religious leaders in the community. I indicated that there was tradition before there was experience, but experience conditioned—or changed—tradition. Both tradition and experience are intertwined in the events of life and each person has to formulate meaning as he or she responds to the events of life. I have no reason to change that general explanation; but it is possible to be more exact about the process and about what kind of religious education is required for developing faith in God.[1]

TRADITIONAL BELIEFS

It is fairly easy to understand the transmission of beliefs. Beliefs are deeply rooted explanation of why the world is as it is, why we act the way we do, and what is important in life. By their very nature beliefs are passed on to children in hundreds of ways each day. Most of our beliefs are thus absorbed as we grow up and become our unargued assumptions about life—unargued, that is, until we are challenged; and then we defend what is "right" from our deeply rooted training.

The Old Testament Shema gives and excellent illustration of the process of transmitting beliefs.

> Hear, O Israel: The Lord our God is one Lord; and
> you shall love the Lord your God with all your heart,
> and with all your might. And these words which I com-
> mand you this day shall be upon your heart; and you
> shall teach them diligently to your children, and shall
> talk of them when you sit in your house, and when you
> walk by the way, and when you lie down, and when you
> rise. And you shall bind them as a sign upon your hand,
> and they shall be as frontlets between your eyes. And
> you shall write them on the doorposts of your house and
> on your gates. Deuteronomy 6:4–9.

The words that are to be taught are, of course, the rules in
the book of Deuteronomy.

But we must not assume that beliefs handed on from
one generation to another remain exactly the same. Beliefs
change slowly to accommodate themselves to new or different social conditions. The festivals of the Jews, for
example, developed over a long period of time and gained
or lost importance according to changing conditions.[2] The
meaning of the Ten Commandments was constantly interpreted and reinterpreted to meet new conditions—as illustrated in the Talmud.

Furthermore, we must not always consider tradition in
negative terms and think that it is restrictive, dogmatic, or
unimaginative. Tradition can be—and often is—all of
these things, but our analysis will be closer to reality if we
think of tradition as an inevitable part of life. All of us are
born into social groups which have beliefs and these beliefs
will be communicated to us from the day of birth. Some
traditions are open-ended; that is, they expect change and
have a way of absorbing change.

The forming and reforming nature of tradition is well
illustrated in the Bible. This tradition had powerful beliefs

which trained each generation; but part of the tradition was an affirmation that God's will is revealed and that obedience to that will is expected. God called Moses to lead the chosen people out of Egypt, but the people preferred slavery with the assurance of regular meals. Amos and other eighth century prophets spoke the word of the Lord for justice; but the people preferred a conventional, unjust society. The gospels present Jesus as fulfilling Old Testament prophecy of a Messiah, thus showing how culture is transmitted; we need not go into details. Our theological and educational problems are related to the other side of the matter. In theological language it is the question: how do we understand revelation? In educational language it is: how do we educate people to expect experiences with God and how do we test and use such experience? These questions have been answered in the Bible. The characteristice form of religious experience is called a theophany. In technical language a theophany is

> a temporal, partial, and intentionally allusive self-disclosure initiated by the sovereign deity at a particular place, the reality of which evokes the convulsion of nature and the fear and dread of man, and whose unfolding emphasizes visual and audible aspects generally according to a recognized literary form.[3]

In less technical language we could say that "a theophany is a temporal manifestation of the deity to man involving visible and audible elements that signal God's presence."[4]

A few illustrations may help. The story of Moses' call to assume leadership of Israel is a central symbol for Jews and Christians. Moses was keeping the sheep of his father-in-law when he experienced God's presence. The voice of God reminded Moses of the "affliction of my people who are in Egypt . . ." and assigned Moses to the task of freeing them (Exodus 3). Later, the whole nation had a tremendous religious experience. Camped before Mt. Sinai, the people saw and heard a dialogue between Moses and God. This was followed by the giving of the Ten Commandments (Exodus 19–24).

Isaiah's experience is a more condensed story. Isaiah apparently had a special relation to King Uzziah, so the king's death made a deep impression on Isaiah. While in the temple, Isaiah was the Lord. All the surroundings trembled and Isaiah's sinful self became real to him. After an experience of forgiveness and cleansing, Isaiah heard God give him instruction as to what he was to say and do for Israel (Isaiah 6).

A scholarly analysis of these and other theophanies may indicate as many as ten characteristics, including a set literary form for describing the experience which set theophanies apart from other types of literature in the Bible.[5] But this paper is not primarily about revelation; it is about how revelation interacts with ongoing tradition. If we look at theophanies from the standpoint of human beings, we may find that there are four major points to consider. A revelatory religious experience is (1) to a person, (2) in a situation, (3) about events that are taking place, (4) directing action towards God's purpose for the world. A brief examination of each of these points will help us think about the nature of an appropriate religious education.

1. To a person. To say that revelation comes to a person means that the individual is the locus of faith and the focus for our endeavors. Furthermore, we can partly describe what a real religious experience is, for we observe in biblical models that the experience was illuminating and

that it made profound changes within the receiver. Through the experience of these people Israel came to understand God's significance for its life. This knowledge of God brought significance to their understanding of God. This conception of knowledge is not synonymous with subject matter; rather it connotes a deeper level of understanding that goes beyond the rational and engages the affections of a person. Thus, to know God in the biblical idiom is closely parallel to the type of knowledge found in the marital relation, a figure of speech which reappears in the New Testament in the description of the church as the "bride of Christ." Subject material about this deep religious experience represents an enduring description of what was true to someone and, by inference, what might become true again to someone else.

2. In a situation. Persons live only in a situation that is timebound and culture-bound. The reality of life is the situation in which people find themselves. It is for this reason we say a revelatory experience is one that comes to a person in his or her situation; otherwise God would have no significance, would not change, modify, or redirect an individual's life. Persons come to awareness and understanding of God through the specific sets of circumstance that operate in their life. In the biblical story we are almost always given an account of the situation through which a revelatory experience comes, because it is as a person changes his or her perception of the situation that he or she obtains a confirmation of God's active presence in life. Thus, there is a "holiness" about each person's situation that causes us to take off our shoes in respect for the concrete reality we face.

3. About events. Events are social and have a reality apart from an individual's situation. Events are constella-

tions of force which move people or to which people react and interact as they organize their corporate life. Events are historical in the sense that we can describe them with a measure of objectivity. Events affect persons, and persons make events. The structure of our community life in industry, government, war, social mores, family, etc., creates events to which we must respond. Again, looking at the Bible, we are struck with the historical character of the Christian faith—historical in the sense that it is directly related to the events it describes. Furthermore, biblical characters who claimed to have the "word of the Lord" always spoke of events which were the common problems of the time.

4. Directing action towards God's purpose for the world. In short, what is revealed in the Bible is God's will for the chosen people. In the Old Testament this is strongly ethical and moral, relating to the covenant with Israel. In the New Testament the ethical is reinterpreted by the concept of God's love, which is demonstrated in Jesus Christ and which is to be reenacted in succeeding generations in the church. The first story of humanity we have in the Old Testament is the failure of Adam and Eve to obey God's will; and in the New Testament the writers refer to Jesus as the second Adam, for he shows humanity more completely and demonstrated perfectly what it means to do God's will. This aspect of the biblical revelation is most difficult for us today. Not only are the events with which we work vastly different from many of those in biblical times, but also it is hazardous to find clear guidance that we can confidently assert is God's will. Nevertheless, to fail to help adults in their areas of decision-making or to omit guidance for contemporary events is to proclaim a partial gospel that can easily become egocentric and sentimental.[6]

LEARNING TO RELATE TO GOD

Since tradition is constantly at work and is already deeply established within us before we are conscious of its presence or power, our educational problem is how to transmit tradition so it can *inform* as well as *form* human experience. Jesus, of course, is our finest example. The Sermon on the Mount is a wonderful example of how he took the intention of the law and applied it to human affairs (Matthew 5–7). In fact, Matthew's way of telling the good news is to show Jesus in opposition to those who were guardians of tradition. The conflict reaches its climax in a confrontation with the Sadducees. Tradition said, "If a man dies, having no children, his brother must marry the widow and raise up children for his brother." This happened to a widow seven times, according to the story, so the question was: "In the resurrection, therefore, to which of the seven will she be wife?" Jesus answered, "You . . . know neither the scriptures nor the power of God. . . . He is not the God of the dead, but of the living" (Matthew 22:23–33). This story is used by Matthew to introduce the famous seven "woe to you" denunciations of those who transmitted tradition but did not practice it nor seek for the living God behind the tradition (Matthew 23).

There are many stories in the New Testament that could be used to illustrate the way a religious experience with Christ changed a person into a "new being." Perhaps the most important one describes how Peter carried over into his Christian life his traditional prejudice against Gentiles. It took an extraordinary vision to get him to see that "God shows no partality, but in every nation anyone who fears him and does what is right is acceptable to him" (Acts 10:34–35). After this experience, Peter allied himself with

Paul, and the Christian religion became open to the whole world.

Trying to relate religious experience to the educational process is our problem. In one sense it cannot be done. We could not, for example, have planned a religious education program which would have brought about Peter's change. But there are some fairly practical things that can be said about the religious educational process which may help us lead people to relate to God.

1. IN TERMS OF OBJECTIVE

There is one major objective in Christian education: helping a person become a Christian. With adults this will mean helping them have the mental and emotional experiences that give them certainty in their relationship to God, plus a growing desire to understand and to do God's will as it affects their lives. For children it will be "faith-in-trust," a leading them to a point where they come to this certainty within themselves.

This general objective presents two problems: (1) We *cannot* describe the quality of this experience of certainty, for it will vary with each person; and (2) we *cannot* say just what persons will do or become as a result of their "growth in grace."

We *can* do four things: (1) We can tell, and in other ways share, what our relation to God is and what that means to us in our situation; (2) we can share what others in the history of Christian faith have known about God and what this meant to the church and to society; (3) we can generalize or speculate as to how God would speak to the person or group with whom we are working, and (4) we can affirm that God is person-like, is open to communication with us, makes redemptive love available to all of us and makes possible a meaningful, shared life with other believers.

The knowledge of God which we wish to share is the certainty of a relationship which is better expressed by faith than by knowledge. The faithful relationship will net us knowledge which we must explain and share but which in itself is not faith. Faith contains knowledge but is deeper and more "inward" than information. In this sense knowledge of faith is instrumental in fostering faith.

Highly specific objectives, which have been suggested in some forms of religious education, came from an educational psychology built on laws of learning formulated on the basis of the memory function of the mind. Shifting to an educational psychology more related to self-conscious selection of goals and more concerned with deep emotional states such as anxiety, hostility, and guilt frees us from measuring results in exact terms. Yet from a practical point of view we must have a plan for our teaching and some general basis for assaying growth. With whatever scheme we use for this practical problem, we should remember these facts: (1) that the general objective is more important than any specific plan or project, (2) that we cannot accurately departmentalize our knowledge of God, since spiritual reality is in event and not in logic, and (3) that the individual and his or her experience is the coordinating factor in Christian education.

2. IN TERMS OF ORIENTATION

Revelation came to us in specific historical situations. It is understood today in the situation we face; therefore, we should start with the situation we face. This involves language, mores, maturity, interest, class, native ability, thought-forms, sex, age, nationality, race, economic conditions, vocation, and religious background. To this people-in-a-situation we seek to relate the gospel. Under some conditions we might start with the gospel or the biblical material and relate that to the persons in the church today; but in either case we must bring about a conversation between these two elements in Christian education.

3. In Terms of Educational Process

American Christian education (up to the last few years) has generally appropriated whatever educational psychology was being taught in the leading universities and has utilized that method for the communication of the Christian message. Although this arrangement has greatly benefited educational processes in the church, it never took seriously the educational process inherent within the biblical message.

The biblical message would cause us to say that the Christian education process is a matter of *understanding* and *participation*. It is a process going on all the time, indicating that a person learns in reacting to the environment. Understanding as used in this context is compounded out of information and the relationship of information to a person and the person's use of information.

Thus, in Christian education we attempt not only to give the facts about the life of Christ but also what these facts mean. Part of this process is made up of rational analysis of information; another part is the pupil's growing insight of himself or herself; still another part would be a comprehension of the realities that face the person in community.

Participation means that the learner responds by living in the life and thought of the church and by undertaking appropriate action in the community. From such participation comes new learning and insight—especially insight into the meaning of God for a person's life; and this in turn drives the person back to obtain more information and knowledge in order to enrich and enlarge his or her conception of the experiences he or she is having.

To see that this process is taking place does not commit us to any one. It subordinates method to purpose and sets the learning process within the context of the living community of believers of the church where affectional responses can be developed and the love of God actualized.

4. IN TERMS OF EDUCATIONAL STRATEGY

It was characteristic of the progressive education movement that it started the educational strategy with children, primarily because they responded readily to that approach. It was done also because of the idealistic impulse which contended that if we could train our children and youth, we could create a new and more satisfactory world when these children grew up and took charge. That conception has, of course, proved to be an illusion; for there is an ongoingness about the world that manages to corrupt each rising generation. The strategy has to be reversed: the Christian education process must be started with adults. Adults have influence in, and responsibility for, culture—the matrix in which Christian education is formed. Practically every known form of revelatory experience has come to an adult who in turn moved out into human affairs to demonstrate his or her concern for God's kingdom. Although our progress with adults will be more modest than with children or youth, what gains we make will be found more permanent.

We must recognize, however, that if we accept this principle we have not necessarily solved our problems, because adult education is extremely difficult. Motivation for learning is the most difficult problem in adult education. Generally speaking, adults do not need skills or information. They already have the basic working repertoire of experience necessary for what they are doing. A child has a native enthusiasm for learning because each new learning experience brings more control over the environment, more pleasure in living, or a better understanding of the world in which he or she lives. Adults have consciously passed through this phase of life and are already reasonably successful in meeting life's problems; they, therefore, have little motivation to learn. Also, adults bring to the learning task their past experiences with learning which in many cases were not good. Some have come to fear almost any new learning situation because they feel so inadequate personally or achieved so little in the real world of affairs. Adults are often afraid of making mistakes. They feel guilty over errors on the assumption that, since they are adults, they are expected to know. Furthermore, adults worry about the waste of time, money, and energy when mistakes are made or accidents occur for they know the value of what is lost. They tend to avoid situations where unpleasantness may occur. Moreover, adults are often reluctant to move ahead in the learning situation because they are acutely conscious of the quality of their work, and they are afraid of the judgments that might be made by friends or by the group if they do not do well.

This quick inventory of the learning situation of adults is

given to show that we are not necessarily doing good adult education when we put more pressure on people to come to existing classes or when we simply broaden the curriculum to include other subjects. Something far more fundamental must be done in adult education. To go back to our biblical model of learning, we must get adults to understand the Christian faith as it applies to them and to their situation in their community. Then we must lead them through understanding to participation so that they will have a certainty of God's activity in the world. We make a mistake when we try to avoid complex issues with adults because motivation rests also on challenge, challenge which is commensurate with a person's or a group's resources.

So much is said about the home and its influence in Christian education that I will not labor the point here except to say that parent education is part of adult education, not the reverse. If we cast our adult education on the basis of parent education, then we have a child-centered adult education program! We must avoid this turn of affairs by making parent education a portion of adult education, a natural corollary of what we do with adults in our church, understanding that education for family living and adult education each support the other and each receive from the other.

5. IN TERMS OF THE EDUCATOR

And now, one final word concerning the teacher, which is an inevitable corollary of the discussion thus far. A teacher's relations to the pupils is one of the most important factors in Christian education. Faith is personal before it is propositional; so we must choose teachers on the basis of what they are as persons first and then in terms of what they can do in the educational enterprise.

NOTES

1. C. Ellis Nelson, *Where Faith Begins* (Richmond: John Knox Press, 1967), Chapter III, "The Dynamics of Religious Tradition."
2. Hayyim Schauss, *The Jewish Festivals* (Cincinnati: Union of America Hebrew Congregations, 1938).3. J. Kenneth Kuntz, *The Self-Revelation of God* (Philadelphia: The Westminster Press, 1958), p. 45.
4. Ibid., p. 17.
5. Ibid., p. 45.
6. Lawrence C. Little, ed., *The Future Course of Christian Education* (Pittsburgh: The University of Pittsburgh Press, 1959), Chapter 16, "Toward Better Methods of Communicating the Christian Faith" by C. Ellis Nelson. The four elements in a religious experience are taken from this chapter.

4

Handing on Traditions and Changing the World

Letty M. Russell

Dichotomies within Educational Ministry

Can the dichotomy of "handing on traditions" and "changing the world" be overcome in Christian religious education? We could answer "yes" to this question by arguing that it is possible to follow the footsteps of George Albert Coe and many others in finding ways the thesis/antithesis is brought together in a new synthesis.[1] Of course, the problem here is not just to find a synthesis, although that is not easy. A more difficult problem is the gap between such a synthesis in theory and in educational practice. We could answer "no" to the question by arguing that dualism is built into human reality and will never be overcome. Dualisms are here to stay: mind/body; spirit/matter; divine/human; male/female; black/white; thought/action. This dualism locks us into certain patterns in social life and theological thought that not only affects educational practice but all of life, as one-half of each pair is assigned greater value than the other.

A third alternative would be to say that the division is wrong in the first place in that the biblical faith is always

expressed in and through actions in history. These actions
are themselves part of the traditioning process and they in
turn are for the purpose of changing the world toward the
vision of God's New Creation. In so far as it is necessary to
postulate dualistic structures, they are symbolic of fallen
creation in which man, woman, and nature are set over
against one another, themselves, and God. They are not
part of the liberating purpose of God's New Creation in
which God has reconciled creatures and creation through
Jesus Christ. As Paul puts it, "When anyone is united to
Christ, there is a new world; the old order has gone, and a
new order has already begun." (2 Cor 5:17, NEB). This
alternative is the one that I would like to argue here, first
reflecting on *educational ministry and tradition* and then on
the clues they provide for the overcoming of some of the
most pressing *dichotomies in educational ministry.*

I. EDUCATIONAL MINISTRY AND TRADITION

Educational terminology in its various shifts and styles
has provided a way of naming what we are doing as
educators in the life of the church. The terms used have
been the descriptive building blocks for holding the various aspects of Christian/religious/education together. For
instance, one can figure out what one means by "religious
education," "Christian nurture," or "Church education" by
analyzing the meaning of the words and then adding them
together.[2] Or one can select a particular word from biblical
or church tradition such as *catechesis, paideia, oikodome* and
go to the root of the word in order to show its correlation
with the totality of what one is about in "equipping the
saints."[3] The words are not important as long as they are
understood by the participants in a conversation. What is

important is the analysis of the meaning of the words and the way they become pointers toward a particular educational or theological position. In taking a position that dichotomies are at the root of our thinking and acting, I want to argue that educational ministry is a more wholistic description of what we are about as we join God in handing on the tradition of Jesus Christ to coming generations and nations.

Educational ministry refers to any form of serving in the name of Jesus Christ that involves us in mutual growth and fuller self-actualization of God's intended humanity.[4] *Ministry* is sharing in the work of the one who came "... not to be served, but to serve ..." and to give his life a ransom for all (Mt 20:28, RSV). In Christian communities the presence of Christ empowers all members of the community for service and not just the women or the clergy. As Rosemary Ruether puts it,

> The principles of Christian community are founded upon a role transformation between men and women, rulers and ruled. The ministry of the church is not to be modeled on hierarchies of lordship, but on the *diakonia* of women and servants, while women are freed from exclusive identification with the service role and called to join the circle of disciples as equal members.[5]

Such service in the New Age is possible, for all persons find their primary identity, not in their assigned sex, race or class, but in Jesus Christ who sets them free for service.

Diakonia, the acceptance of someone else's life project as our own scenario or story, begins with accepting Jesus' own story as our own and then extends to solidarity with others. Acts 6:1–6 makes it clear that the early church saw

the deacon as a "waiter on table." Certainly it is a word
without much glamor: "Functioning as a waiter, that is, to
be subordinate, to be inconspicuous, to be available, ready
to give a hand."[6]

Education is a process of actualizing and modifying the
development of the total person in and through dialogical
relationships.[7] Ministry is educational when it offers the
possibility of growth in ability to serve others. In one sense
all ministry is educational whether or not this is intended,
for human beings learn from their social environment
through the enculturation process. We learn through participation in a faith community which communicates the
meaning of ministry which is practiced in that community.[8] In another sense ministry can be intentionally educational when there is a process of partnership in learning,
so that persons of all ages are invited to join in God's
continuing actions.

Describing one's educational intentions as Christians as
"educational ministry" has the possibility of beginning beyond the dichotomies of ministry/education; clergy/
educators; teachers/students; public education/church
education. As Christians we all share in Christ's ministry or
service, and we are all involved in a life long process of
partnership in learning to serve in Christ's name.

Handing on the tradition is another description of educational ministry, for God is the one who does the "handing
on" or traditioning (*parádosis*), through human communication of one person or group to another. As Congar puts
it:

> Tradition, like education, is a live communication whose
> content is inseparable from the act by which one living
> person hands it on to another.[9]

Through the Spirit God continues to minister or serve and equips us so that we may grow in our commitment (Eph 4:12). God's traditioning action has often been dichotomized in the past so that in the history of the church we hear of scripture versus tradition or of the traditions of God versus the traditions of men, and so on. Yet more and more theologians have come to a consensus that tradition can be understood in at least three different ways.[10]

The first meaning, indicated here by the word *Tradition* with a capital "T," is the biblical understanding of the dynamic and continuing process of God handing over Jesus Christ into the hands of all generations and nations. In this sense Tradition is not a static deposit (*paratheke*) to guard or a once delivered faith (1 Tim 6:20; 2 Tim 1:14; Jude 3). Rather it is a dynamic action of relationship or handing over as described in Matthew 17:22 and Romans 8:31–32.

Another meaning, indicated by the word *tradition* with a small "t," is a basic anthropological category of the structural element of human existence in which the still living and evolving past calls for commitment in shaping human community in the present and future.[11] Human beings are "time machines." They live in the present, remembering the past and envisioning the future. In a world of change they live in all three times by means of selecting the elements of the past most usable for the present and future.

The last meaning, indicated by the word *traditions* with an "s" on the end, refers to the many and various religious traditions that have grown up over a period of time within our cultures, subcultures, and confessional communities. These traditions are an important part of our own identity and that of groupings of people. They are bearers of the gospel message in various situations. However, they are

not of ultimate significance in relation to how we might
want to live out our faith, and they tend to divide us when
taken so seriously that we declare other traditions to be
heretical. We need to be aware of our own traditions and
to look for those that need to be changed, as well as for
those what can form a usable past.

These three forms of tradition are not contradictory.
They simply indicate in an oversimplified way that the
word *tradition* is used in various ways, so that we can be
clear what we mean when we talk about "handing on tradition" and "changing the world." God's Tradition in which
we participate continues to be handed on through the continuing witness to Christ and it certainly is a liberating
dynamic of change in the world. The human process of
traditioning is certainly both continuing and causing
change by its very definition as a continuing process by
which we select from the past to shape the future. The
church traditions that aid us in locating the meaning of
the gospel in a particular context and faith community
may or may not continue to be handed on or contain a
dynamic of change. Such distinctions are helpful in overcoming false dichotomies within educational ministry.

II. OVERCOMING DICHOTOMIES

The word *dichotomy* refers to being cut-in-two. Human
beings observe reality, and seek to abstract it into ordered
patterns. Often these patterns represent a dualistic approach to reality in which things are typed in opposite
pairs. These dichotomies in our thinking are at the root of
the malaise of our culture and theological traditions. We
stereotype things and people and assign them meaning,
value, and roles in ways that are dehumanizing and non-

functional for full human development. In particular we have used this dualism to justify racism and sexism, inventing dualisms that assign the qualities of public power, strength, and intellect to white males and the qualities of service, emotional weakness, and bodily needs to women and blacks. Jean Baker Miller reminds us that:

> Finally, these formulations are themselves a reflection of the whole dichotomization of the essentials of human experience. The present divisions and separations are, I believe, a product of culture as we have known it—that is, a culture based on a primary inequality. It is the very nature of dichotomization that is in question.[12]

Such dualism weakens everyone in their full growth and human potential and hinders the development of an educational ministry that is truly good news for all parts of society.[13]

In the practice of educational ministry such dualistic attitudes lead to dichotomies that defeat the possibility of full participation in God's sending and saving actions. For the dichotomies appear not only in sex and race stereotypes, but also in the assumptions behind our educational approaches. Three dichotomies that need to be reinterpreted in the light of handing on tradition *in order to* change the world toward God's New Creation are: action and thought; education and theology; church and world.

Action and thought have often been cut-in-two in the history of religious thought. When Coe tried to eliminate "the dichotomy between knowing and doing ... by merging Christian doctrine with Christian experience" this was but one of a constant series of attempts to bring together faith and works, revelation and experience, reflection and ac-

tion.[14] We know the two have to come together for, as
Freire points out, thinking without action is verbalism, and
action without thinking is activism.[15] Yet educationally we
find great difficulty in moving from theory to practice or
vice versa. Action deals with particulars that are carried
out in personal or social activities, while thinking deals
with universals or general statements.[16] There is no one
way to move from thought to action or action to thought.
This is perhaps why Freire places such stress on praxis as a
continual feedback process of action and reflection that
has no beginning or end. His pedagogy is one of learning
to question one's world and to take action together with
others to change it.[17] This in turn leads to new questions
and experimental actions. As means of moving beyond the
dichotomy, praxis seems more effective than the method
of teaching content without providing any experience in
learning to think or act in relation to that content or doctrine.

One way to address this dichotomy in terms of understanding tradition is to say that Tradition understood as
God handing over Jesus Christ into the hands of coming
generations and nations includes both action and thought
in the process itself. We are caught up in the ongoing story
of Jesus Christ and by living out that story in our lives
invite others to share in that action of God. When tradition
is understood as a deposit or block of content a dichotomy
immediately results, for one then hands over the content
and expects others to go out and make sense of it in their
lives. Usually the actions are shaped by the social context
and life experience that may or may not have anything to
do with the content.

Handing over Jesus Christ as a person in a living relation among persons is not any easier, but at least action

and thinking are united in the effort to share one's whole existence with Christ in service to others. The aspect of faith most easily seen as a point of entry for this type of learning is *assensus*: consent to action/participation in God's Traditioning. When we view educational ministry as an opportunity for young and old alike to try out the life story of Jesus in their lives and to discover what this commitment means the dichotomy between action and thought is taken up into one process of God's action.

Education and theology are constantly represented as a dichotomy in the life of all church educational institutions. Christian educators work hard to spell out the two components and their interrelation. Often the error is made of falling back on our first dichotomy so that, as Moran puts it, "theology supplies the content and education provides the method."[18] This ignores completely the fact that both education and theology have commitments to theory and practice that need to be well correlated if educational ministry is to be more than an imitation of public schooling or academic institutions.

This dichotomy is also promoted by the understanding of tradition as a block of content. When this is the assumption, then theology can equal content or doctrine that has been accumulated in the past as "banking theology" and teaching/learning becomes the way theology is dispensed through a variety of educational methodologies. However, when tradition is understood as the still living and evolving past by which we shape the future then we discover that education and theology are both part of tradition. They are part of the process of learning to choose critically from the still living and evolving tradition in order to shape the future in the light of God's intention for justice, liberation, and wholeness for all.

As God continues to hand over Christ into our lives we
receive the gift of faith in a variety of ways. The Reformers
described these interrelated aspects of faith as *assensus,
notitia,* and *fiducia.*[19] As I have already indicated, *assensus* is
a beginning point for the interrelation of thought and action in the context of life experience and commitment. In
the human process of tradition, *notitia* also becomes an
important methodological clue. *Notitia* is taking notice of
God's actions; of the story of God with Israel and in Jesus
Christ and the church. The story will remain alive as the
possible integrating point of education and theology, if we
allow it to be told over and again in different ways so that
both the theology and the education are shaped in the
sharing of that story of service.

Church and world represents a dichotomy that is to be
seen in many forms in the life of the church; a dichotomy
that serves to defeat the purpose of educational ministry as
growth in ability to serve others in all parts of the world.
The same dichotomy is to be seen in many "either/or's"
such as: preacher/teacher; clergy/laity; religious/secular.
Too often we think of everything in the church as part of a
sacred sphere, cut off from the profane. This form of
dualism is enhanced by the trend of secularization that has
assigned religion to the private sphere along with women
and children. Yet if God's action is concerned for total
humanity, the church is called in all aspects of its life to be
the part or that world that points critically toward God's
intended New Creation. There is no division of two worlds
with clergy living in the "unreal" spiritual world and laity
in the "real" world.[20] Church practices that contribute to
this cripple educational efforts in equipping the *whole*
people of God for their work of caring and protest in the
name of Christ.

This dichotomy as it affects educational ministry can be addressed from our perspective on the meaning of *traditions* as the way in which we incarnate the gospel message in particular cultures and confessional traditions. In dichotomous thinking of "we/they," traditions are used as barriers between church and world. They are the way a particular cognitive minority establishes its identity over against others, and defines the way in which it will act. Such separation works as long as the cultural tradition and ethos of the church is strong enough to make it what Berger has called a "plausibility structure."[21] What is taught is also made plausible as a way of life by the community handing on the faith. But in a pluralistic society, everything seems to become more and more relative or watered down because people convey the impression that nothing matters. Yet true pluralism is made up of many groups that are convinced that *something really matters* and this is the intention of traditions in which Christ matters.

Traditions make it possible for the church to situate itself as those who serve Christ in the midst of the world, because they are the way we live out the gospel in a particular context so that all in that context may come to know both its risk and promise. It is persons whose lives are a living reminder of the meaning of ministry who are the main plausibility structure of education. Hannah Arendt reminds us that even Socrates did not know how thinking could be taught. He only knew that he could infect people with the same perplexity that he felt.[22]

Fiducia operates in the same way. As an aspect of faith, *fiducia* is the gift of complete confidence and trust that enables us to hope against hope that God loves us. It is not taught, but caught. Traditions help a community to be Christ's agents in the world. They make the gospel come alive in the life style of persons so that others may become infected with faith. But they may become a barrier between groups within, among and outside of Christian communities when they cease to point beyond themselves to Christ and become ends in themselves.

In educational ministry we no longer need to divide things into *either/or*, for "handing on tradition" and "changing the world" are both what God's Tradition is all about. We participate in God's handing over of Christ through continued action in the world, and invite others to come along with us. Our ministry as Christians will include critical struggle against the world as it is, in favor of God's New Creation. Such ministry will be in itself a partnership in learning; a process of self-liberation in community with others.

As the Final Assembly of the World Council of Christian Education in Lima, 1971 said:

> To educate is not so much to teach as it is to become committed to a reality in and with people, it is to learn to live, to encourage creativity in ourselves and others; and under God and [God's] power, to liberate [humanity] from the binds that pervert the development of God's image.[23]

As Christians and humanists we can no longer afford dichotomies of *either/or*. Instead we are drawn into God's reconciling action toward God's intended future where we can speak of *both/and... More to Come!*

NOTES

1. Susan B. Thistlewaite, "Education and Covenant," *New Conversations* 2:2 (Fall, 1977), pp. 16–20.

2. Neil G. McClusky, *Catholic Education Faces Its Future* (Garden City: Doubleday and Co., 1968), pp. 27ff.

3. Malcolm L. Warford, *The Necessary Illusion* (Philadelphia: United Church Press, 1976), p. 55; cf. Ian A. Muirhead, *Education in the New Testament* (New York: Association Press, 1965).

4. Charles E. Melchert, "What is the Educational Ministry of the Church?" *Religious Education* (July–August, 1978).

5. Rosemary Radford Ruether, *New Woman, New Earth* (New York: The Seabury Press), p. 66.

6. Hans Hoekendijk, *Horizons of Hope* (Nashville: Tidings, 1970), p. 30.

7. Letty M. Russell, *Christian Education in Mission* (Philadelphia: The Westminster Press, 1967), p. 28.

8. Warford, *Illusion*, pp. 53–55; John Westerhoff, *Will Our Children Have Faith?* (New York: Seabury Press, 1976), p. 50.

9. Yves Congar, *The Meaning of Tradition*, trans. A. N. Woodrow (New York: Hawthorne Books, 1964), p. 28.

10. Letty M. Russell, *Human Liberation in a Feminist Perspective— A Theology* (Philadelphia: The Westminster Press, 1974), pp. 73–78

11. Gerhard Ebeling, *The Problem of Historicity* (Philadelphia: Fortress Press, 1967), pp. 37–45.

12. Jean Baker Miller, *Toward a New Psychology of Women* (Boston: Beacon Press, 1976), p. 79.

13. Maria Harris, "Isms and Religious Education," *Emerging Issues in Religious Education*, G. Durka and J. Smith, eds., (New York: Paulist Press, 1976), p. 43.

14. Thistlewaite, "Education and Covenant" p. 18; cf. George Albert Coe, *What is Christian Education?* (New York: Charles Scribner's Sons, 1929), p. 29.

15. Paulo Freire, *Pedagogy of the Oppressed* (New York: Herder and Herder, Inc., 1970), pp. 75–76.

16. Hannah Arendt, "Thinking III," *The New Yorker*, Vol. LIII:42 (Dec. 5, 1977), p. 205; cf. C. Ellis Nelson, *Where Faith Begins* (Richmond: John Knox Press, 1967), p. 20.

17. Freire, *Pedagogy*, pp. 64, 66.

18. Gabriel Moran, *Design for Religion* (New York: Herder and Herder, 1970), p. 21.

19. Henrich Heppe, *Reformed Dogmatics* (London: George Allen and Unwin, Ltd., 1950), pp. 530–534.

20. Barbara Brown Zikmund, "But I have called you friends: A Theology for the Laity in the United Church of Christ" (Office of Communication, UCC Eleventh General Synod, June 30–July 5, 1977, Washington, D.C.). Unpublished speech.

21. Peter Berger et al., *The Homeless Mind* (New York: Random House, 1974), p. 184. Quoted by M. Warford, *op. cit.,* 36.

22. Arendt, "Thinking III," p. 136.

23. *Work Book for the Fifth Assembly of the World Council of Churches* (Geneva: WCC, 1975), p. 40.

5

The Language of Religious Education

Dwayne Huebner

During the conference itself, my task was well defined and manageable—to respond critically to each paper as it was presented to the conference participants. Given each paper's consistency of content and method, I had little difficulty identifying one or more critical perspectives which would illumine or bring under question method and/or content. The diversity of the papers posed no special problem because their totality did not have to be acknowledged.

But a written response to the papers does pose a problem. The reader senses some kind of unity or need for unity among the four. They are diverse in method and content, but surely there is some form or structure that holds them meaningfully together. They are part of a much larger dialogue about Christian religious education. The reader should be able to recognize how one paper related to another; how one challenges the assumptions of the others.

Furthermore, social endeavors that are reasonably autonomous and disciplined are usually accompanied by appropriate forms of criticism which provide the negative thrust and the articulation of value necessary for the continual transformation of the endeavor. Christian religious education appears to lack that coherency and disciplined autonomy. There appears to be no larger perspective to give a semblance of unity to the four papers and to permit ready and constructive criticism of each paper and its relationship to the other papers.

The diversity of the papers points to this lack of unifying form or structure. In fact, the diversity is an invitation to search for a form which will provide at least a semblance of coherance for the four papers. The written challenge is to transcend the discreteness of the four and to forsake the easy way of responding to each paper independently. The written response should be a contribution to the ongoing construction of the edifice within which religious educators can work and talk about their work.

The core of our problem is that we are concerned with two phenomena which permeate most aspects of our existence, but which defy rigorous and disciplined objectification in language: education and the religious. The linkages between our language about education and the religious and our experiences of education and the religious are tenuous and ambiguous.

We might like the security of the linkage between language and phenomena associated with the scientific-technical endeavors; but that security is impossible. These endeavors are constructed out of the controlling interests and capabilities of the human being. The scientific-technical linkage is based on our ability to transform phenomena, or at least to predict regularities so transformation becomes a possibility if the technology develops at a later time. Transformation and prediction in education and the religious are not necessarily attainable. If we work under the illusion that they are, we frequently distort and more often destroy the experience, for power over and social control of the other person is the usual result. In this age of science and technology, we are uneasy with ambiguity of the linkage between the language and the experiences of education and the religious. Uncomfortable with that ambiguity, we take known, but partial, ways and substitute a segment for the totality. Because we have learning theories—scientific-technical endeavors which can transform internal and external conditions related to learning—we assume that education is a manifestation of learning. Because we have used sociological and anthropological methods to develop sociologies and anthropologies of religion, we assume that these methods give us an adequate language link with religious phenomena. Because we have theories of socialization, we assume that these provide adequate language links for the experiences of education and the religious.

Failing to find security in the presumed objectivity of the scientific-technical endeavors, some of us hope to establish the link between language and the experiences of education and the religious by a turn to the subjective. The social values of poetry, private journals, and other objectifications of the subjective in works of art are clear. They can be significant works, which link language to one person's experiences of education and/or the religious. As expressions of personal experiences of others, they provide a contrast with my experience and a critical contrast with the objective world. But they also have their limitations. One person's experience of education and of the religious is, at best, a limited and fallible guide for creating contexts within which others can experience education and/or the religious. We aspire to something more public and socially useful, beyond the use value of works of art, poetry, journals, and other objectifications of the subjective.

We need a public language, as we need public buildings, public gardens, public transportation, public ceremonies. These public spaces, public means, public occasions provide grounds upon which we meet. They are the grounds for community. The public resources position us in our meetings with others. They offer orientation as we observe others work and listen to them speak. They give us directions as we do things together. They often give shape and meaning to our personal experiences, or a ground against which we can compare our personal experiences.

A public language for education and the religious should resonate with and articulate our personal experience. It should provide a perspective as we watch others engage in religious education and as we listen to them speak about their experiences and contexts of religious education. Furthermore, it should provide a sense of direction as we live educationally and religiously with others.

Yet our need for a public language should not be permitted to cover the tenuousness and the ambiguity of the link between language and education and/or the religious: it should acknowledge them. Whereas the public language may alleviate the tendency to retreat into the subjective, it does not alleviate the tendency to fall forgetfully into the objective—into the otherness of language which is presumed to have truth value, that can only be partial; or a normative force, that can only be disguised social control.

The presence of public language in the speaking and writing of others makes it easy for us to forget that it is ours, or that it can be ours if we choose to participate in it. It is not yours, or theirs, or mine. But it is ours only if we assume responsibility for it. It is something that we jointly construct, or jointly maintain—and in its construction and maintenance we construct and maintain ourselves. Thus we should not let linguistic meanings dominate us unless they are our meanings too. We should not accept the rules governing the uses of language unless we can accept the rules as ours. In this sense, public language is not normative for us, rather it fits the way that we are and want to be in the world with others—it does not demand that we be in it in a particular way. The responsibility for and the mutuality of construction and maintenance are stressed to counter the social division of labor in our society, the impact of the scientific-technical in our lives, and the ease with which we forget the origins of that which we have taken on as our own—we forget our predecessors who share the public domain with us.

These conference papers illustrate all three of these points. Developed societies have created specialization to cope with the diverse functions that exist within these societies. One of the functions that has been separated out is the responsibility for the development, maintenance, and criticism of the language resources of the society. Thus, there are those who sharpen the social use of language and attempt to define, linguistically, our social and personal life. These functions have been the domain of the academic and media specialist.

Professor Nelson claims that "Christian education as a field of study and research is rather new; in America it began about 1900 and rapidly became important in our major universities and seminaries." The turn of the century is also a time that marks the beginning of the disciplined study of education and the rapid increase in university specialists who labored to increase the "knowledge of" education. "Knowledge about" is, primarily, the "lan-

guage of" education. Increasingly, the language changed
from a public language to a would be scientific-technical language, produced and criticized by specialists, primarily university academics, and distributed among the
users or the practitioners by books and college courses.
Practitioners assumed less and less responsibility for the
language used, and became more dependent upon the ex-
pert. Today, the theory-practice split is not, primarily, a
split of theory and practice, but a social split between those
who educate and those who assume responsibility for the
production, maintainance, and criticism of the language of
education. If we possessed better historical studies of the
development of specialization in education they might
show that the increasing alienation of educators from their
language and eventually from the students and the experiences of education is related to the growth of the scientific enterprise, which, while supposingly supporting education actually controls much of it.

With this displacement of the responsibility for the construction and maintainance of language to a specialized
labor force, and the increased significance of the scientific-technical as a model for that language, we tend to
forget that language is a production of particular people in
particular circumstances. This in turn leads to the neglect
of the origins of language, and to the failure to recognize
that the use of someone else's language carries responsibilities. The first responsibility is to recognize that interpretation is a constitutive part of language. The meanings
and uses of language are never absolute. They always require interpretation by the users. The second responsibility is to recognize that the use of someone else's language
makes us historical agents. We are the sources of historical
continuity or discontinuity. Our predecessors, those who
used our language before us, are also part of our public.

I am not aware of studies which depict the development of religious education in relationship to the development of education in general, but surely the relationship must be a close one. The study of education and the study of religion require methods which increasingly came under the domination of the social and cultural "sciences."

This conference is a manifestation of the social division of labor and points to our problems of historcal responsibility and continuity. The papers were prepared and responded to by members of the academic community. The audience, in large measure, were practitioners of religious education. The latter came to listen and to raise questions of the academics, perhaps to interpret their language. The trend that started at the turn of the century is now institutionalized into roles and social hierarchies. Groups of experts, usually university faculty, are frequently drawn together to attempt the reformulation of religious education, which means to produce more useful language with which a variety of people might talk about religious education and to establish the linguistic boundaries and definitions of the field. What do we know about how the practitioners of religious education speak about their work and their experiences, or how the students speak about their experiences? The division of labor, constructed and reinforced over the past several decades, means that those who partake of religious education infrequently participate in the construction or criticism of the public language of religious education. They await the pronouncements of the specialists. Furthermore, the specialists infrequently attempt to describe how language is used by the practitioners, or to describe the work of the practitioner. This neglect is common to education in more secular domains as well.

These four papers, and the response, must be seen as

contributions to the ongoing construction of the edifice within which religious educators can work and talk about their work. This is not a work for specialists, although specialists surely must participate. This is a work for all who are concerned with and who experience religious education as educators or educatees. That academics are engaged in writing and responding to these papers makes the language no less fallible and no more normative than if someone else wrote or responded. We can expect from specialists more disciplined method in the criticism and transformation or reconstruction of that language which aims toward being "public," just as we can expect from practitioners more disciplined methods in the transformation of the social environment within which religious education occurs. Both should be equally accepting of the tenuousness and ambiguity of the language-experience linkage, and accept with great caution language which bases its claim to legitimacy on the scientific-technical endeavors, or expressive-artistic endeavors.

These disciplined methods of criticism and transformation or reconstruction must be appropriate to the resources that we have—namely, the language which is already part of our ground as Christian religious educators. We are not starting a new enterprise. The language ground that we have is already an historic ground—our predecessors are part of our public. Therefore a major method for transformation and criticism must be historical—the discipline which articulates historical continuities in the uses and interpretation of language.

Furthermore, the language ground within which we stand was not always constructed with the public in mind. It might have been constructed by specialists, with their interests in view. Previous divisions of labor are still operative, even though they may no longer be functional in this day and age. So the second major method must be a critical method—one which disciplines us to center and de-center, and enables us to bring under question our own interests and those of others. A critical method does not take the present distribution of power and of specialization as being permanent or fixed, but seeks to lay bare the social relationships underlying that which is and to enable us to see from multiple perspectives.

The method that I will employ to illumine and question the papers is one which seeks to expose the basic framework of the edifice needed to make public our work of religious education and the talk about that work. The first problem is to identify the language tools by which the authors articulate educational and religious phenomena. If we accept the proposition that there can be no one to one correspondence between language and the experiences of education and the religious, that there is a built in ambiguity, then the task is not one of identifying truths about either education or the religious, but of identifying the way in which those phenomena are objectified in language.

The second problem is to identify the origins of that language and to begin the search for the historical continuities and discontinuities in the language use. This task is merely one of pointing to the kind of work that must be done more thoroughly in the future, for I lack the needed historical competencies. The lack of well exposed historical roots in education in general, and religious education in particular, indicates that most of us lack the much needed historical competencies to identify the predecessors who are part of our public.

The third problem is one of centering and de-centering.

We must be able to de-center from our own language uses, to get away from our taken for granted ways of speaking and thinking and consider the possibility of speaking about phenomena as others do or as others might if they could give voice to their experiences. We do this by asking whether existing relationships among differing groups are being unconsciously maintained. Hence the de-centering is the act of negation, which brings under question the taken for granted realities or our natural attitude. The recentering is considering other possibilities as possibilities for us.

The final problem is to identify the work that needs to be done—the kinds of historical and critical work which must be brought to bear upon existing language if we are to move to a more useful public language for religious education.

The order of the work is to consider first, the problem which served as the unifying theme for the conference papers. Next, the educational dimensions of the papers will be considered and then the religious dimensions will be brought under scrutiny.

THE CONFERENCE THEME

The unifying theme of the conference, "Christian Religious Education: Handing on Traditions and Changing the World," posed the problem for each author. Boys solved the problem by stipulating a definition of education as "making accessible." Christian education, seen as providing access to religious traditions and to human and social transformation, is shown to be consistent with biblical sources as these have been interpreted by biblical theologians. Harris considered three terms that she identified with Christian tradition—word, sacrament, and prophecy. She suggested that religious educators embody these in acts of teaching, hallowing, and parable. She proposed that if we look at the educational and religious dimensions of each of these acts, then any split between handing on traditions and changing the world is healed. Nelson solved the problem by identifying it as continuous with the biblical circumstances wherein the revelations of God seemed to bring under question the existing traditions of belief and practice. He then used modern educational language to suggest how we could create contexts for religious education today. Russell saw the problem as part of our human propensity for dualisms. Accepting the tradition of Jasus Christ as central to our mission of education, she suggested that if we interpret our task as one of handing on the tradition of Jesus Christ, as a problem of educational ministry, then the dualisms can be overcome. Nelson indicated the roots of the conference theme in biblical experience. Russell suggested that a Christocentric focus would provide the necessary reconciliation. Boys suggested that the starkness of the polarity as identified by Coe, and by segments of particular church communities was inconsistent with the interpretations in modern biblical scholarship. Harris left the historical roots more or less undisturbed.

The theme of the problem is rooted historically, in the Bible for instance; and the language has its origins within biblical language and theological reflection about that language. The problem is, as Russell states, a reflection of the "structural element ef human existence." We are temporal beings with a past, present, and future. Tradition refers to our memory of the past, in language, artifacts, customs, and institutions. Education is something that we do in the present. Transformation is a concern for the future. How do religious educators, educatees, and laity experience the possible conflict or reconciliation between tradition and transformation, between past and future? There is no question that the theme has been kept alive, in writing and speaking, in the works of theologians, educators, and other academics. Certainly Coe articulates the liberal optimism of the mid-progressive era, when transformation seemed a viable option and education a viable vehicle. As we academics experience the traditionalism of schools and other institutions and as we dream of our desired transformation, our language and our teaching serve as political actions to bring about transformations of those institutions. Does the language of the teacher or of the students express the contradictions and limits that the academics sense? Does the language of curriculum writers, community leaders, or laity express these contradictions, polarities, and reconciliations? Do they share the political and institutional commitments of the academics? Are we, the academics, solving our own problems or are we articulating a language that can be used by the practitioners to solve theirs? Whereas three of the authors have pointed to the historical continuity of the theme, none has defined the social parameters of the theme. We remain unaware of whether the people in various religious education communities see religious education, their presence and present with the young, as a problem of bringing together the handing on of traditions and the changing of the world. In fact, we remain unaware of the problematics faced by religious educators. Thus, we have no way of knowing whether the theme is an expression of merely an academic community, which identifies its own historical continuity with Coe and the carriers of biblical concerns, or whether it is indeed an expression of educators and educatees in a variety of settings.

THE LANGUAGE OF EDUCATION

How is the experience of education articulated in the four papers? What are the possible sources or historical precedents of these ways of talking about education? Are the various articulations brought under critical scrutiny to identify taken for granted interests? What work needs to be done to make the articulations useful and valuable to all involved in religious education? In raising these questions we must heed Russell's warning of the possible dichotomy between education and theology, wherein education provides the process and theology or religion the content. We wish to call attention to the experiences of education not simply the process of education, and the many ways in which those experiences have been articulated, just as we wish to call attention to religious experience and the many ways that they have been articulated. In doing so, we do not mean to imply that these experiences of education and of the religious are distinct and must be considered separately; only that there are dominant traditions that tend to keep them separate.

In fact, Harris's paper is an attempt to reunite those very separations to which we have been accustomed. Whereas she speaks of education in more or less individualistic psychological language as the "growth and development of the human," and the educational problem as the technical one of designing "an environment in such a way that others are put in touch with their own resources and the resources of the environment," she tries to maintain the

unity of education and the religious by speaking of the
three gracious acts of teaching, hallowing, and parable.
But she does not hold the unity, for she identifies the
educational dimension of these three as naming, ordering,
and questioning. In so doing she points to these aspects of
education that are characteristic concerns of educators—
language, meaning, doubt, or negation. The problem that
she encounters is one of the methodological and substan-
tive deficiencies in the study of education. Those experts
who should have the most disciplined methods for criticiz-
ing and transforming educational language have not, as
yet, applied these methods to the way we speak about the
place of language in education, the function of doubt and
negation in the educational process, or the relationship
between personal meaning and social or institutional
meanings. However, because she does not seek out her
historical predecessors, in a sense does not identify the
historical work that needs doing, she identifies only her
contemporaries and she speaks of her own experience.
She verges on the poetic and names her own experience,
her own meanings. Her language might indeed resonate
with the experiences of the practitioners, but we do not
know. Her language must also be placed in historical
perspective. She needs to establish that the acts of religious
educators can indeed be described as "gracious acts" of
naming, ordering, and questioning. Can the activities of
practitioners be so neatly categorized? Without this historical and de-centering work. Harris's language of education
can either float over the educational experiences of other
or become unnecessarily normative for them.

Boys also breaks with dominant language traditions as
she speaks of education as "making accesible." She em-
phasizes the mediating function of education and points to

the exemplars that come to mind when one refers to how access is obtained. Unfortunately, Boys also fails to establish the direct connection between the language of education and the historical precedents, but the failure verges more on the objective side than on the subjective side. Again, the failure is not hers, but a failure of those who are presumably most capable of using disciplined methods to criticize and transform educational language. Russell refers to the possible basis of religious education in the sociology of knowledge and critical theology, and in her bibliographical reference to Schillebeeckx (n. 21) she points to the work of Gadamer and Habermas. Her definition, then, serves to bring into the discourse of education tools from the sociology of knowledge and its predecessors of the Frankfurt School of Critical Sociology and of various Marxists concerned with the distribution of cultural resources. But without the identification of predecessors, readers are left to their own interpretation and are lost or not located historically. The practitioner's interpretation of "accessibility" must be personal, for they are not helped to see how all educators, past and present, have participated in the distribution of various cultural resources. However, the potential power of this definition is suggested in her paper. The work that needs to be done is to describe how the activity of all religious educators provides or restricts access to resources or experiences of others. That the practitioner may be unaware of providing or restricting access is a function of the language which describes education in psychological or individualistic terms. Boys's language, then, offers the possibility of seeing education as a dialectical experience between the person and the socially constructed world. However, the dialectical nature of education is only suggested, not developed, and the dialectical method as an educational method for relating past and future to the present is not developed. Somehow, this articulation of education as dialectical needs to be constructed to resonate with the experience of practitioners, so they not only see, but feel their activity as mediating activity, and as necessarily limited by social and institutional structures. If this construction is appropriately done, then religious educators will more easily recognize their participation and complicity in the maintaining and transformation of institutional and social structures. Boys's suggestion that we provide access via proclamation, narration, and interpretation is surprisingly close to Harris's concern for naming, journey, and questioning.

Harris and Boys push us into other ways of articulating the educational and risk falling into the subjective or unconsciously into other historical continuities usually ignored by educators. Nelson and Russell on the other hand, maintain relative continuity with the predominant educational language of today, although it must be acknowledged that their discourse is primarily about religious experience. Boys's term "access" is helpful for analysis. Russell is concerned with providing access to the "Tradition of Jesus Christ." Nelson is concerned with providing access to traditional beliefs and to revelational beliefs. How is access to be provided?

Russell defines education as the process of actualizing and modifying development of the total person in and through dialogical relationships." and states that "human beings learn from their social environment through the enculturation process." She clearly recognizes that education of the individual requires participation in a community that lives "religiously" and does not merely talk or

teach about doing so. Education is a consequence of enculturation, participation, praxis, of "trying on the life story
of Jesus." For her, ministry is a way that past becomes
future in the present.

Nelson's paper illustrates more clearly the choices of the
religious educator when confronted with the ambiguous
link between language and experiences of education and
the religious. He establishes that the distinction between
traditional beliefs and revelational beliefs, or religious traditions and religious experience, has biblical origins. He
accepts the work of the social and behavioral scientist and
states that "with our modern knowledge of how culture is
transmitted, we need not go into details [about tra-
ditions]." Appropriately, he acknowledges that we have a
problem when we consider education and "revelation beliefs" or religious experiences. "How do we educate people
to expect experiences with God and how do we test and
use such experiences?" He returns to the theology of revelation and an analysis of theophanies to identify some basic
dimensions of religious experience. Later in the paper he
states that "Trying to relate religious experience to the
educational process is our problem. In one sense it can't be
done." Recognizing the need of practitioners for "practical
things that can be said about the religious educational
process which may help us lead people to relate to God,"
he draws upon more or less typical educational language.
The unclear bridge between the analysis of theophanies
and the "practical things" is a manifestation of the basic
ambiguity.

Russell and Nelson are both articulate about the biblical
precedents of their educational concerns, but they in-
adequately establish the historical precedents or the critical
perspectives of the educational language. Both recognize

that education "happens" or "occurs" to adult and to children, yet the educational relationship between adults and children is interpreted as one of enculturation, socialization, or transmission. When and under what auspices did we begin to frame educational experience this way? Again we lack the necessary historical perspectives of educational discourse. The incorporation of social and behavioral science terminology is relatively recent in education. It began slowly at the turn of the century, was increasingly emphasized during the scientific movement in education in the twenties, and has been accepted without reservations since the fifties. Yet the interests of social and behavioral scientists are not neutral and until very recently reflected a naive positivism—and acceptance of the given social phenomena as the only reality. Recent interest in the history of childhood[1] increases our awareness that the way we talk about children is historically conditioned and may indeed influence how we interpret education today. Increasingly, the socialization paradigm is also being brought under question as one which hides the taken for granted realities and interests of adults in maintaining the status quo.[2] Nelson tacitly acknowledges this as he proposes that Christian education "must be started with adult" because "Adults have influence in, and responsibility for culture." Who, then, "educates the educators" and how can adults be certain of their understandings and ways of being in the world?

The work of Piaget, his genetic epistemology, provides one of the major de-centering methods for adults. Piaget has demonstrated that some of our presumed epistemological problems are a consequence of looking at knowledge only in the operation of adults. By observing the development of knowledge in infants and children he has fundamentally reconstructed our understanding of the relationship of knowledge to the body. The emphases of Nelson and Russell point to the need for a kind of Piagetian de-centering from adult conceptions of the religious in order to see more clearly the possibilities of Christian religious education. Russell's concern for "ministry," "serving," and "sharing in the work of one who came" provides a powerful focus for Christian religious education. One way that we prevent distortion of our conception of ministry and service are adult acts of responsibilities. Piagetian de-centering forces us to ask about the basic "structures" of service and ministry in the adolescent, the child, and perhaps the infant. Do we, in fact, have difficulty with educational ministry because our adult ways of being in the world have already covered over and displaced or distorted basic forms of ministry and service which develop easily in the neophyte, if we only have the eyes to see and the ears to hear? Are the processes of enculturation and socialization mechanisms by which basic tendencies toward ministry and service are lost in most adults? Are socialization and enculturation mechanisms by which the past in the lives of adults takes precedence over the possible transforming actions and questions of the un-socialized—the child?

Nelson's concern for revelational beliefs and religious experience also carries with it possible adult biases. In fact, he makes the claim that "Practically every known form of revelatory experience has come to an adult." Perhaps this is the case because we adults do not value the experiences of children, or would not recognize a revelatory experience or a religious experience in a child? A Piagetian de-centering would push us to question our understanding of revelation as an adult phenomena and force us to observe and listen to the young more carefully and with greater criticism of our adult perceptions and conceptions.

Part of the needed work, then, in our construction of a

more public language for Christian religious education is based upon accepting the centrality of ministry and revelation or "religious experience" in religious education. But we do not recognize the work that needs to be done if we simply accept our present educational language and describe presumed social and cultural mechanisms by which a person "learns" or "develops" forms of ministry or by which adults "live and teach their most cherished beliefs in such a way that children learn to relate to God" [Nelson]. Our language should be constructed to be descriptive of the life of the young as well as the life of the adult. Such language could change the perceptions and conceptions of adults and fundamentally alter our ways of being with the young educationally. We need a "developmental or genetic ministry" and a "developmental or genetic theophany." Such theological disciplines might shed light on the cultural and social forms which distort, impede, or block the development of Christian life.

THE LANGUAGE OF RELIGION

The review of some of the educational issues touched on the articulation of the religious in the four papers. These articulations need to be placed in historical and critical perspectives and the next steps or needed work in the construction of a more useful public language of religious education should be identified. My own disciplined methods are not appropriate for the critical review of the language of the religious, hence I can only suggest questions which should be asked of the papers.

Again, both Nelson and Russell write within existing theological contexts: Russell within the context of Christology and Nelson within the context of the theology of revelation. Their interpretations need to be placed in historical and critical perspective by theologians who can comment on their theological warrants. But the structural problem of the specialization of labor in the religious community can be raised again. What are the possible relationships among the ways that practitioners of religious education, educatees, and laity speak about Christ, ministry, and revelation. What social functions are Nelson and Russell serving as they write about these aspects of the religious? Are they mediators between the practitioners and the theologians? Are they merely agents of transmission? Do the concerns and language of lay educators and educatees ever critique the language of theologians and if so do Nelson and Russell serve as two way agents of transmission and mediation?

Boys speaks more directly to these series of questions. Among other things her paper demonstrates the use of a particular theological method—biblical criticism—to illuminate aspects of religious education. Although she makes some recommendation for practical action, her major work is to demonstrate that control of a disciplined method can be used by religious educators to rethink their commitments and practices. Biblical criticism is a method for thinking about the relationship between past, present, and future. She also suggests that one possible function of the religious educator is to serve as a mediator between theologian and pastors, educators and the people. Russell speaks to the same problems, in slightly different terms, as she discussed the dichotomies of church and world, education and theology.

Harris speaks of the religious from a less clearly defined perspective. The religious dimension of her three gracious acts—journey, sacrament, and foolishness—do not parallel existing disciplines, although there is much work on the theology of symbol and sacrament. A theology of story is taking form,[3] which reflects Harris's interest in journey. But she does not establish the link with either of these bodies of reflection. In a sense, she writes from a perspective opposite to that of Nelson, Boys, and Russell, and hence illustrates, by reverse image, the same problem. She does not write from an established theological ground. Let us assume that she writes from the ground of a practitioner of religious education who dares to give language form to her own experiences. She attempts to have the form match the disciplined experience of teaching rather than match the disciplined methods of one responsible for the criticism and reconstruction of language.

As I pointed out earlier, we are not sure that Harris's language would resonate with other practitioners. However, if we were to ask other practitioners to articulate what they do or want to do would they be as independent as she has been, as able to give form to the complexity of religious education? How should one disciplined in the methods of theology respond to her language and how should she respond to theirs? The mutual neglect of each others work and language identifies the structural problem in our efforts to build a public language of Christian religious education. Can the sources of this language be theologians, academics, and practitioners, and what responsibility do they have to each other? The missing ingredient in Harris's paper, however, is the lack of historical continuity. The historical continuity is easily maintained by theologians because of their training and the way that the discipline is made "accessible." The same is not true of practitioners, who more often than not practice in an historical vacuum. Is this because they lack a sense of the historical or because the means of access to their descipline or work filters out the historical? Does their contact with the cultural pluralism that they find among their students force them to articulate their affinity with other traditions, thus, unfortunately breaking down, rather than reconstructing their own historical continuities with their predecessors? Why is it that Harris, writing more as a practitioner even though within an academic setting, ignores the Christological foundations and the theology of revelation?

The contrast between the papers of Nelson, Russell, and Boys and that of Harris points to a major structural problem in Christian religious education. The social structure which should bring together in common cause those who work as religious educators, whether with the language of religious education or the practice of religious education does not exist or exists in imperfect form. How can the communities of the religious be transformed to reconcile the rift between the interests of theologians, the practitioners, the educatees, and the people?

CONCLUSION

Theologians, academics, religious educators, and laity share responsibility for the way they give voice to our educational experiences as religious people and as Christians. Could some of the difficulties and problematics of the practice of Christian religious education be associated with our collective failure to share responsibility for this collective voice, this needed public language? Has the specialization of labor made the practitioner voiceless but practically

powerful in that they maintain institutional forms;
whereas the theologian and academic are "voiceful" but
powerless to change institutional life? Is this the hidden
theme of the conference? Is "handing of tradition" seen as
a function of language and "changing the world" seen as a
function of institutions? The reconciliation cannot occur at
the level of language alone, unless language is also seen as
an embodiment of institutional life. We should ask not
only about the meaning of language, but about the social
organization which structures the use of language and its
relationship to practical activity. We cannot be concerned
merely with the way practitioners speak, think, and
practice in an isolated institution. We must be concerned
with the interlocking relationship among the many institutions which are involved, in various ways, with religious
education. Has the development of universities and
seminaries somehow interferred with the development,
criticism, and transformation of language resources in
churches and local institutions? Are teaching, writing, and
conferences the best link between the language disciplines
of experts and the institutional disciplines of practitioners?

One way to begin a restructuring of these relationships
is to begin to make more public the voices of practitioner
and educatees. How do they articulate their educational
and religious experiences and problems? What do they
make of the academics and theologians. Because academics and theologians are in positions of educational power, the disjunction between what they say and think and
that which others say and think is often interpreted as
educational deficiency. The criticisms of the young and
the laity can be put down as uninformed. Is this educational hubris? There is no easy solution. The reverse demand that academics and theologians get their hands and

feet dirty in practice can be mere tokenism. Who should possess poetic power, the disciplined method for historical perspective, the critical discipline for de-centering, the political and imaginative disciplines of transformation? Where should those who possess these disciplines reside and how should they exchange their productive work with others?

The problem is structural and political, not simply one of knowledge and language. How are ministry, revelation, tradition, transformation, and the word welcomed, practiced, and criticized wherever they are found—in all of life's situation and social institutions? How do we hear the past and see the future whenever we speak and work? Can our biblical and other religious traditions inform and form us as we transform the relationships among the many institutions within which we live and serve?

NOTES

1. E.g. Philippe Aries, *Centuries of Childhood*, (New York: Random House, 1962), and Lloyd deMause, ed., *The History of Childhood*, (New York: The Psychohistory Press, 1974).
2. E.g. Hans P. Dreitzel, *Recent Sociology No. 5: Childhood and Socialization*, (New York: Macmillan, 1973).
3. [Editor's Note] On the theological uses of story and journey see, for example: John Dunne, *Time and Myth: An Exploration of Storytelling as an Exploration of Life and Death* (Garden City: Doubleday, 1973); John Shea, *Stories of God* (New York: Macmillan, 1978); Harvey Cox, *The Seduction of the Spirit* (New York: Simon and Schuster, 1973). For the application of these concerns for religious education see Thomas H. Groome, "The Crossroads: A Story of Christian Education by Praxis," in *Lumen Vitae* 32 (March), 1977.

Index